"The work of being both C
challenge. While not all readers will follow ....
all who read it carefully will come away strengthened in their faith ..
their ability to use the mind faithfully for the service of God. Read, ponder,
and read again."

—MARK A. NOLL, Francis A. McAnaney Professor of History,
University of Notre Dame

"When Charles Malik trumpeted his clarion call to save the mind as well
as the soul, it was 1980. Malik, always a prophet, statesman, and Christian
intellectual, was ahead of his time, and few had ears to hear his challenge.
But times have changed. This is not just another Christian book on the
mind. It is a wake-up call that should be read by all Christians interested
in the world of ideas and apprenticeship to the Lord Jesus."

—J. P. MORELAND, Distinguished Professor of Philosophy,
Talbot School of Theology, Biola University

"Charles Malik ranks with C. S. Lewis, Carl F. H. Henry, Harry Jellema, and
Arthur Holmes in his perception of the critical role of the university in culture
and of the desperate need for serious Christians to engage in the academic
enterprise. Every Christian professor in every academic discipline should
read every essay in this book. It could transform the way they understand
their role in the university. That could transform the university and thereby
transform culture."

—JAMES W. SIRE, author of *The Universe Next Door* and *Habits of the Mind*

"Thirty years ago, with rare exceptions, it was difficult to find outspoken
Christians in the Western intellectual world. Today the growing number
of evangelicals and committed Catholics now found in secular academia
may be viewed as a reflection of the vision of Charles Malik. This volume
does an excellent job of describing the current status and dreams of the
Malik vision."

—HENRY F. SCHAEFER III, Graham Perdue Professor of Chemistry,
University of Georgia

"Charles Malik's trumpet call from the steps of the Billy Graham Center in
1980 reverberates again. The formidable task of saving souls and minds is
no less urgent, perhaps more so. But here we have hope evidenced. These
authors see change, good change, blowing in the universities of the West.
Read this call for courage, perseverance, and may God's scholars take up
the charge in our generation."

—LON ALLISON, Director Billy Graham Center,
Associate Professor Wheaton Graduate School

"This does justice to the dignity and brilliance of Malik and to the greatness of Jesus Christ as our world's only hope."

—KELLY MONROE KULLBERG, author of *Finding God at Harvard*

"Craig and Gould have brought together an outstanding group of scholars, offering stimulating insights and interesting nuances. This volume is a rich source of ideas, challenge, and inspiration for all seeking to serve the kingdom as Christian academics."

—STAN W. WALLACE, National Director, InterVarsity's Faculty Ministry

"Christians have invested much in the task of evangelism and discipleship on university campuses. Meanwhile we have neglected the nexus of influence in the university, the classroom itself. This generation must take seriously Malik's challenge by not merely ministering on the periphery of the campus, but by enabling well-credentialed godly women and men to teach at secular universities. Then we will fulfill Malik's call and the challenge of this volume to proclaim the Lordship of Christ in the epicenter of our culture—in the university classroom."

—DARYL MCCARTHY, President, International Institute for Christian Studies

"This inspiring collection of essays builds on and seeks to apply Malik's original lecture across the disciplines. Readers will be inspired to give their lives to the great work of integrating faithful Christian living and witness with all that happens in and through the University.

—GREGORY E. GANSSLE, Yale University, Rivendell Institute

THE
Two Tasks OF THE
Christian Scholar

REDEEMING *the* SOUL,
REDEEMING *the* MIND

William Lane Craig
and Paul M. Gould, EDITORS

FOREWORD BY HABIB MALIK

CROSSWAY BOOKS
WHEATON, ILLINOIS

The Two Tasks of the Christian Scholar: Redeeming the Soul, Redeeming the Mind
Copyright © 2007 by William Lane Craig and Paul M. Gould

Published by Crossway Books
    a publishing ministry of Good News Publishers
    1300 Crescent Street
    Wheaton, Illinois 60187

Cover design: Jon McGrath
First printing 2007
Printed in the United States of America

Unless otherwise indicated, Scripture references are from *The Holy Bible: New International Version®*. Copyright © 1973, 1978, 1984 by International Bible Society. Used by permission of Zondervan Publishing House. All rights reserved.

The "NIV" and "New International Version" trademarks are registered in the United States Patent and Trademark Office by International Bible Society. Use of either trademark requires the permission of International Bible Society.

Scripture quotations marked KJV are from the *King James Version* of the Bible.

All emphases in Scripture quotations have been added by the author.

"The Two Tasks" by Charles Malik is reprinted with permission from EMIS/BGC, P.O. Box 794, Wheaton, IL 60189; E-mail: emis@wheaton.edu; web site: www.billygrahamcenter.org/emis.

In chapter 4 by Peter Kreeft, quotations from *A Christian Critique of the University* by Charles Malik (copyright © 1987 by John North) are used by permission of North Waterloo Academic Press.

Library of Congress Cataloging-in-Publication Data
    The two tasks of the Christian scholar : redeeming the soul, redeeming the mind / William Lane Craig and Paul M. Gould, editors ; foreword by Habib Malik.
        p. cm.
    Includes bibliographical references and index.
    ISBN 978-1-58134-939-9 (pbk.)
    1. Learning and scholarship—Religious aspects—Christianity. 2. Education (Christian theology) I. Craig, William Lane. II. Gould, Paul M., 1971– . III. Title.

BR115.L32T86 2007
268—dc22
                                      2007018702

VP		15	14	13	12	11	10	09	08	07
14	13	12	11	10	9	8	7	6	5	4	3	2	1

CONTENTS

Contributors

Walter Bradley is Distinguished Professor of Engineering at Baylor University, where he is developing a global poverty center to integrate appropriate technology (School of Engineering), social entrepreneurship (School of Business), and missions (Truett Seminary) to facilitate a holistic Christian ministry to the poor in developing countries. He came to Baylor from Texas A&M University where he was a highly successful professor and head of the Department of Mechanical Engineering, helping his department develop into one of the best in the nation. Additionally, during his twenty-four years at Texas A&M, Dr. Bradley served as director of the Polymer Technology Center, and received five College of Engineering research awards. He has received over $5 million in research grants and has published over 140 refereed articles in journals and conference proceedings and fifteen book chapters, including six in the area of faith and science. He has also co-authored *The Mystery of Life's Origin: Reassessing Current Theories*. He is a Fellow of the American Society for Materials and of the American Scientific Affiliation and serves as a consultant for many Fortune 500 companies.

William Lane Craig is a research professor of philosophy at Talbot School of Theology in La Mirada, California. He earned a doctorate in philosophy at the University of Birmingham, England, before taking a doctorate in theology from the Ludwig-Maximilians-Universität München, Germany. There, he was a Fellow of the Alexander von Humboldt-Stiftung for two years. Prior to his appointment at Talbot he spent seven years at the Higher Institute of Philosophy of the Katholike Universiteit Leuven, Belgium. Dr. Craig has authored or edited over thirty books, including *The* Kalam *Cosmological Argument*; *Assessing the New Testament Evidence for the Historicity of the Resurrection of Jesus*; *Divine Foreknowledge and Human Freedom*; *God, Time, and Eternity*; and *Reasonable Faith*, as well as over a hundred articles in professional journals of philosophy and theology, including *The Journal of Philosophy*; *New Testament Studies*; *American Philosophical Quarterly*; *Philosophical Studies*; *Philosophy*; and *British Journal for Philosophy of Science*.

Paul M. Gould is a doctoral student in philosophy at Purdue University. He earned an MA in Philosophy of Religion and Ethics from Talbot School of Theology in December 2003. His research interests include metaphysics, philosophical theology, apologetics, and the integration of the Christian worldview within academia. His passion is to promote a robust and viable picture of the Christian world and life to the academy and the culture at large. Paul serves with Faculty Commons, the faculty ministry of Campus Crusade for Christ, as an Academic Initiative field representative.

Robert Kaita is Principal Research Physicist in the Princeton Plasma Physics Laboratory (PPPL) at Princeton University. At PPPL, he is head of Plasma Diagnostic Operations for the National Spherical Torus Experiment (NSTX). He is also Co-Principal Investigator for the Lithium Tokamak Experiment (LTX). Both NSTX and LTX are devices for fusion energy development, and Dr. Kaita's research focuses on the use of liquid metals as a "first-wall" material for fusion reactors. In the Plasma Physics Program of the Department of Astrophysical Sciences at Princeton University, Dr. Kaita has supervised the research of nearly two dozen graduate students. He also serves as the faculty advisor for the Princeton Graduate InterVarsity Christian Fellowship. Dr. Kaita has nearly three hundred publications in nuclear and plasma physics. He is a member of the American Association for the Advancement of Science, a Fellow of the American Physics Society, a Fellow of the American Scientific

Affiliation, and a member and past president of the Princeton Chapter of Sigma Xi, the Scientific Research Society.

Peter Kreeft is a professor of philosophy at Boston College and adjunct professor of philosophy at the King's College, New York, NY. His primary fields of interests are philosophy of religion, ethics, C. S. Lewis, and philosophy in literature. After graduating from Calvin College, he earned an MA and PhD from Fordham University before receiving a Sterling Fellowship at Yale. He has taught full time at Boston College since 1965. Dr. Kreeft is in wide demand as a speaker and is a frequent contributor to several Christian publications including *First Things*, *Christianity Today*, and *Crisis*. He is the author of fifty books on philosophy and apologetics, including *Christianity for Modern Pagans: Pascal's Pensees*; *Making Sense Out of Suffering; The Journey: A Spiritual Roadmap for Modern Pilgrims*; *C. S. Lewis for the Third Millennium*; *Socrates Meets Jesus; Between Heaven and Hell*; *The Unaborted Socrates*; *The Best Things in Life; and Handbook of Christian Apologetics.*

Habib Malik is Associate Professor of History and Cultural Studies at the Lebanese American University (Byblos campus) in Lebanon. He is also the only son of the late Lebanese philosopher, diplomat, and devout Christian, Charles H. Malik. Habib Malik graduated in 1985 from Harvard University with a PhD in modern European intellectual history. His own spiritual journey is one of the chapters in Kelly Monroe's book, *Finding God at Harvard*. In addition to the university where he currently teaches, Dr. Malik has served on the faculties of the Catholic University of America in Washington, DC, and the American University of Beirut (off-campus program). Dr. Malik was a visiting Fellow at The Washington Institute for Near East Policy in 1995 and 1996 and a visiting scholar at the American Enterprise Institute in summer 2003. He divides his interests between the history of Western thought and the issues and problems of his ancestral home, Lebanon, and the Middle East at large—in particular the plight of native Christian communities, the future of freedom and democracy in Arab societies, and the challenges posed by Islamization. He is the author of *Between Damascus and Jerusalem: Lebanon and Middle East Peace; Receiving Soren Kierkegaard: The Early Impact and Transmission of His Thought*; and he is editor of *The Challenges of Human Rights: Charles Malik and the Universal*

Declaration. In addition, he has published many articles, essays, and book chapters, in both English and Arabic, on a variety of themes related to his interests. Finally, Dr. Malik is president and CEO of the Charles Malik Foundation, a nonprofit organization registered in the United States, and a founding member of Lebanon's leading independent human rights NGO, the Foundation for Human and Humanitarian Rights.

John North is Professor of English at the University of Waterloo, Ontario. Educated at the University of British Columbia and the University of Alberta, he has been Killam Post-Doctoral Fellow at the University of British Columbia (1971), Senior Visiting Research Fellow at Queen's University Belfast (1981), and Research Fellow at the Institute for Advanced Studies in the Humanities at the University of Edinburgh (1983). At the University of Waterloo he was cofounder of the Pascal Lecture Series on Christianity and the University and recently received the Distinguished Teacher Award. His research interests are Victorian literature, children's literature, literature and the Bible, and bibliography. In 2006 the Society for the History of Authorship, Reading, and Publication gave him the annual Award for Distinguished Achievement, citing his thirty-four-volume *Waterloo Directory of English [& Irish, & Scottish] Newspapers and Periodicals, 1800–1900* as "one of the great feats of humanities scholarship in the modern era." He has edited books on poetry and on computing in the humanities, a well as several volumes of the Pascal Lectures on Christianity and the University, including Donald Mackay's *Science and the Quest for Meaning*; Charles Malik's *A Christian Critique of the University*; Malcolm Muggeridge's *The End of Christendom*; Josef Pieper's *What is a Feast?*; and Margaret Avison's *A Kind of Perseverance*.

FOREWORD

My late father, Charles Malik, would have been very comfortable among evangelicals. In fact, he was totally in his element spiritually among and within all the great traditions of Christianity—Protestant, Catholic, and Orthodox. He would have thanked the Lord Jesus for each of these groups, the true salt of the earth.

Born February 11, 1906, in a remote village in an obscure corner of the then Ottoman Empire, a place that was to eventually emerge as the tiny Republic of Lebanon, Charles Malik went on to leave his mark on the world's stage in more than one field:

- His early studies in natural science and mathematics in which he excelled and which provided him with a grounding that served him well throughout his life.
- His later lifelong concentration on philosophy, after studying under both Alfred North Whitehead and Martin Heidegger, arguably the two philosophical giants of the twentieth century.
- The contributions he made in the areas of human rights, international diplomacy, Christian ecumenism, academia,

the cause of a free Lebanon, U.S.-Lebanese relations, and much more.

But surely the most important and abiding feature of the man, the real clue by his own admission to his success and his positive influence, was the strong faith in Jesus Christ that he received at an early age as a gift from God through his grandmother in whose bed he slept every night for twelve years as a youngster. He lived this faith through the feasts and festivals of the Orthodox church in his home village in north Lebanon where he assisted at Mass as an altar boy every Sunday throughout those formative years. And this is also the most precious gift that he and my late mother have passed on to me—the gift of faith in the Lord Jesus.

For those who knew him personally, Charles Malik's physical appearance, his height, the large distinctive head (one friend once likened it to that of the Old Testament prophet Jeremiah, as if he had ever seen Jeremiah!), and the unmistakably deep and resounding voice—all left a lasting impression on anyone who met him. He exuded a powerful charisma through an imposing presence, and at the same time he could be jovial, gentle, pleasant, and humble.

Many, like Eleanor Roosevelt who worked closely with him at different stages of his public career at the United Nations, found they could rely on his judgment and wisdom as well as his persuasive powers of argumentation. Others were profoundly inspired by his spiritual depth and sincerity. On September 19, 2006, before the United Nation's General Assembly, President George W. Bush found it appropriate to mention him twice at the outset of his speech and in the context of human rights: "The principles of this world beyond terror can be found in the very first sentence of the Universal Declaration of Human Rights. This document declares that the 'equal and inalienable rights of all members of the human family is the foundation of freedom and justice and peace in the world.' One of the authors of this document was a Lebanese diplomat named Charles Malik, who would go on to become President of this Assembly. Mr. Malik insisted that these principles apply equally to all people, of all regions, of all religions, including the men and women of the Arab world that was his home."

Whether in the way he lived and spoke or in his writings on Christian themes, Charles Malik's first and foremost love was what he called the life of the mind and the spirit—hence the two tasks that preoccupied him so much. All his life he wrestled with the need to enrich this rigorous intellectual existence through immersion in the practical day-to-day challenges of the world of politics and diplomacy, while he simultaneously sought to shield the mind and the spirit from the many distractions that come with the responsibilities imposed by constant involvement in the concrete affairs of the world.

His reluctant entry—and it was reluctant—into politics, locally in Lebanon and then on the world's stage at the United Nations and in Washington, and the deflection that that represented from the quiet contemplative and scholarly life of sheltered academia is something he agonized over repeatedly in his letters to close friends, in the privacy of his personal diaries, and of course, with my mother on a continuous basis. Eventually, he learned to harmonize both worlds (as much as possible), and what is more significant, to remain faithful to Christ in both capacities. No small feat!

As Mary Ann Glendon of Harvard Law School puts it in a poignant tribute entitled "The Layperson in the Public Square: Lessons from the Life of Charles Malik,"[1] his life as a Christian in the public sphere embodied three distinct lessons: (1) God's plan for your vocation may be different from yours; (2) finding your vocation does not mean you will find comfort; and (3) we may never see the most important fruits of our vocations in our sojourn here on earth.

On this third lesson that Mary Ann Glendon mentions, Charles Malik was the tenacious warrior against communism for over forty years and the one who almost single-handedly took on the powerful ideology of the mighty Soviet Union, both at the United Nations and in speech after speech everywhere he went, predicting confidently the sure demise of such an empty and inhuman system. Yet Charles Malik passed away at the tail end of 1987, just short of seeing his predictions fulfilled at the collapse in 1989 of the Berlin Wall and the subsequent unraveling of communism. So the third lesson is of course true.

Perhaps Malik's contributions to the ecumenical rapprochement of the Orthodox, Catholic, and mainline Protestant churches will stand out in the future as one of his greatest legacies. He himself embodied this ecumenism. He was at the same time Greek Orthodox to the marrow of his bones and loved the rich liturgy of that church;

---

1. Mary Ann Glendon, "The Layperson in the Public Square: Lessons from the Life of Charles Malik," *Sacerdos*, July–August 1999, 7–15.

he also steeped himself in the medieval scholastic Roman Catholic theologians and thinkers like Thomas Aquinas and others; and he had a very special, life-long, intimate relationship with the Bible, which he read daily according to a rigorous schedule, a practice that endeared him to Protestants. In our family, thanks to him, we lived a very openly inclusive and accepting form of ecumenism among all three Christian traditions. Two of his brothers (my uncles) became Roman Catholic priests—one a Jesuit and one a Dominican—and my mother's side of the family is largely Protestant Congregationalist.

People ask me, what was it like growing up the son of a great man? My answer is, it was great! But only so because Charles Malik never let greatness detract from fatherhood. I learned from him so many things: my faith in Christ, a certain discipline in life, seriousness in ultimate matters, a love for the life of the mind, important basic distinctions, proper prioritizing, and the ability to recognize the devil's work when confronted with it. I say I learned these things, but I continue to make mistakes in all of them. I know, however, where I learned them from. I also learned much more, including how to be a loving and tender father to my own three children, Eva, Charles, and William, and a dedicated husband to my wonderful wife, Hiba.

Above all, for me Charles Malik was that wonderful and loving father. Who could ask for more? I feel very blessed, and I thank the Lord constantly for this gift that remains undeserved. The time with him on this earth was too short, and he and my mother never saw my three children. But of course as Christians we live in the Christ-given hope of the eternal reencounter with our loved ones who have gone to him before us.

It is a fitting commemoration of Charles Malik's centenary to honor his memory with a volume that aptly focuses on the *Two Tasks'* message. A number of the contributions in this volume attempt to situate this seminal concept within specific academic contexts that their respective authors have experienced firsthand. Paul Gould begins by placing the *Two Tasks* within the framework of a fully integrated life in academia. Robert Kaita reflects on the *Two Tasks'* theme as a scientist working at Princeton on the cutting edge of research in physics. Walter Bradley considers the challenge posed by the *Two Tasks* in being a Christian professor at the secular academy. John North does the same with a particular focus on what it means to live the two tasks as a professor in the humanities. For his part,

philosopher Peter Kreeft broadens the scope by pulling into the
discussion Charles Malik's other major work on spirituality and the
academy, *A Christian Critique of the University*, and he masterfully
probes where we would have been today had we taken that book's
challenge more seriously. My own contribution attempts to outline
a contemporary set of issues facing the Christian believer caught
in the midst of the ongoing clash of civilizations and how all this
relates to the original *Two Tasks*. Lastly, William Lane Craig offers
some insightful parting thoughts on what it means to be a committed
Christian academic.

The Malik family will always be grateful for this tribute in the
form of a festschrift of love and appreciation compiled by fellow
Christian believers who were touched by Charles Malik in their
thoughts and lives.

Habib C. Malik, PhD
Associate Professor of History and Cultural Studies
Lebanese American University (Byblos campus)
November 13, 2006

1

THE TWO TASKS INTRODUCED:
THE FULLY INTEGRATED LIFE
OF THE CHRISTIAN SCHOLAR

PAUL M. GOULD

> *"All that is good, all that is true, all that is beautiful,*
> *all that is beneficent, be it great or small, be it perfect*
> *or fragmentary, natural as well as supernatural,*
> *moral as well as material, comes from Him."*
>
> —John Henry Newman, *The Idea of a University*

The impulse of modern society is to compartmentalize our lives. Public/private, sacred/secular, work/play, and so on. Modern man and modern society has lost its spiritual center, becoming fragmented and hurried—but only God knows what for! In this cultural milieu, the Christian scholar who bravely resists this impulse toward fragmentation finds the situation exacerbated due to two countervailing pressures that often pull in opposite directions. On the one hand, the secular ethos of the university presses Christian scholars to conduct their research and teaching in purely secular terms and motifs. If Christian scholars want a place at the table, they must play by the rules of the academic game. A strict wall of separation between church and state exists, and any effort to tear down the wall is looked on with either suspicion or outright incredulity. On the other hand, the Christian scholar is committed to a particular view of the world that is often quite antithetical to the established secular ethos. The Christian universe is a God-centered universe. If Jesus is Lord, he is Lord of all areas of thought and life. In fact, the Bible claims that in Jesus "are hidden all the treasures of wisdom and knowledge" (Col. 2:3). Thus, the Christian scholar himself often becomes disintegrated, compartmentalizing his "scholarly life" from his "spiritual life" as he attempts to navigate between the Scylla of religious fundamentalism and the Charybdis of accommodationism. Any attempts to invoke a Christian perspective to science (for example) in the university are quickly labeled as fundamentalist attempts to promote religion masquerading as science. Any attempts to utilize non-biblical conceptual schemes erected by thinkers such as Plato, Aristotle, or Kant in order to shape and guide research and teaching are (sometimes) viewed by the church as selling out to accommodationism. The net result of these opposing pressures is that the Christian scholar is left in a sort of "no-mans land"—viewed with suspicion by both the church and the university. And within the secular academy, religion is relegated to the sidelines. Religion is reserved for the scholar's personal life: meaningful to either the individual or one's own religious community only.

Is it possible to live an integrated life within secular academia today? Can a Christian scholar integrate his faith with his chosen discipline in such a way as to avoid the charge of either fundamentalism or accommodationism? Charles Malik thought so.

On September 13, 1980, the great Lebanese ambassador and Christian statesman Charles Malik (1906–1987) joined Billy Graham and ten thousand others for the dedication of the new Billy Graham Center at Wheaton College. With passion and prophetic vision, Malik implored Evangelical Christians in America to engage in two great tasks: "that of saving the soul and that of saving the mind."[1] Malik warns:

The problem is not only to win souls but to save minds. If you win the whole world and lose the mind of the world, you will soon discover you have not won the world. Indeed it may turn out that you have actually lost the world.[2]

1. See page 64 in chapter 2.
2. See page 63 in chapter 2.

Malik understood that the heart cannot receive what the mind cannot entertain, and thus a key component in reaching our world for Christ must include helping people first imagine a world where Christianity is real. No one cares much today about what Zeus thinks regarding the nature of human persons or what the Flat Earth Society (it really does exist!) has to say about the physics of space-time. Christianity hovers dangerously close to this irrelevance if the life of the mind is neglected inside the church and the truth of Christianity is not defended winsomely and rigorously outside the church.

But for academics and the university, Malik has a special challenge. He realized that as the university goes, so goes the world:

> All the preaching in the world, and all the loving care of even the best parents between whom there are no problems whatever, will amount to little, if not to nothing, so long as what the children are exposed to day in and day out for fifteen to twenty years in the school and university virtually cancels out, morally and spiritually, what they hear and see and learn at home and in the church. Therefore the problem of the school and university is the most critical problem afflicting Western civilization.[3]

Ideas have consequences, and the university in general and professors in particular are the gate-keepers of ideas—influencing directly or indirectly all aspects of thought and life in our world. Christian professors must live a fully integrated life even in the face of challenges from within and without, for the sake of the lost—and as Malik states, for our future generation of children.

Malik did not have in mind a soft and tame Christian scholar within academia. What is called for is something perhaps, dare I say, radical—not radical to God, but radical to *us* in this day and age where it is expedient to conform and fit in:

> I assure you, so far as the university is concerned, I have no patience with piety alone—I want the most rigorous intellectual training, I want the perfection of the mind; equally, I have no patience with reason—I want the salvation of the soul, I want the fear of the Lord.[4]

---

3. See page 60 in chapter 2.
4. See page 60 in chapter 2.

Malik is not content, nor is Christ, with a compartmentalized life. *Soul* and *mind*, united together and flowing into helping *hands* (or in academic speak, a ready pen or clarion voice), is the call of Christ to the Christian professor within secular academia. Being the best chemist, engineer, historian, or whatever for Christ is certainly part of the story—but this cannot be all; we must give people Christ—for what else is there really? Again, Charles Malik believed Christian scholars could live integrated lives within academia.

Faculty Commons, the faculty ministry of Campus Crusade for Christ, agrees.[5] In the summer of 2006, in the centenary year of Dr. Malik's birth, Faculty Commons held its biennial National Faculty Leadership Conference seeking to honor and renew Malik's call to these two great tasks of redeeming the soul *and* redeeming the mind. Through much interaction and lively debate among over four hundred Christian faculty, the idea of a book addressing the two tasks for our day and age emerged.

The following essays touch on one or both of these great tasks, seeking to apply Malik's message to the current context and situation within the halls of secular academia and the culture at large. But before we get to these essays, I propose to lay some groundwork to prepare us for what lies ahead. In this introductory chapter, I first will highlight the state of Christian scholarship within secular academia since Malik's address over twenty-five years ago. There has been progress as well as many encouraging highlights along the way. But, as we shall see, there are still many challenges—both from *without* in the form of active hostility or a general apathy and marginalization of Christianity and from *within* in the form of a lack of vision and a general tendency with academics (and Christian scholars are not immune to this tendency) to "go it alone" without paying attention to one's spiritual well-being. Second, I will attempt to locate Christian scholarship and the integrated life within the context of God's story as communicated though Scripture. Often it is not just the secular person who has lost his center, but it is the Christian, who after years of specialized study within a narrow discipline has lost the forest for the trees. We must learn to fit our story into God's larger story—what he is doing in redemptive history—if we are going to accurately *understand* and *apply* the

---

5. In May of 2007, the faculty ministry of Campus Crusade for Christ changed its name from Christian Leadership Ministries to Faculty Commons.

two redemptive tasks listed by Malik. Third, armed with a general understanding of the metanarrative of Scripture, I will proceed to define in more concrete terms what an integrated life might look like for the Christian scholar in secular academia. And finally, I shall introduce each of the forthcoming essays in this book within the context of this fully integrated life.

Christian Scholars in the Academy Since Malik's Two Tasks Address

In this admittedly cursory highlighting of the state of Christian scholars and scholarship in the academy since Malik's address, I want to begin by noting three important works (representative of many more of like kind) that have served as rallying points for discussion and calls to action: one example from my own discipline, philosophy, and two examples from historians, writing generally to all Christians or Christian scholars.

First, in his November 4, 1983, inaugural address as the John A. O'Brien Professor of Philosophy at the University of Notre Dame, Alvin Plantinga argued that Christian philosophers in particular and Christian intellectuals in general must display more autonomy, more integrity, and more courage in living out their Christian commitments within academia.[6] Plantinga argues that it is perfectly fitting for the Christian scholar to *start* from what he knows as a Christian when engaging in research. By allowing Christian assumptions to inform the scholarly enterprise, Christian scholarship will sometimes look different than its secular counterpart—informing the principles and procedures adopted in the *doing* of scholarship as well as the very questions asked and research programs undertaken. And we should not apologize for this:

My plea is for the Christian philosopher, the Christian philosophical community, to display, first, more independence and autonomy: we needn't take as our research projects just those projects that currently enjoy widespread popularity; we have our own questions to think about. Secondly, we must display more integrity. We must

6. Alvin Plantinga, "Advice to Christian Philosophers," first published in *Faith and Philosophy* 1, no. 3 (October 1984): 253–71. Page references hereafter are from James Sennett, ed., *The Analytic Theist: An Alvin Plantinga Reader* (Grand Rapids: Eerdmans, 1998), 296–315.

not automatically assimilate what is current or fashionable or popular by way of philosophical opinion and procedures; for much of it comports ill with Christian ways of thinking. And finally, we must display more Christian self-confidence or courage or boldness. We have a perfect right to our pre-philosophical views; why, therefore, should we be intimidated by what the rest of the philosophical world thinks plausible or implausible?[7]

Plantinga argued in his own style and with much chutzpah that Christians need to integrate their faith into the scholarly enterprise. And as we shall see in a moment, by and large, Christian philosophers (at least) have heeded Plantinga's advice.

Second, present at Malik's 1980 address was Mark Noll, then a Wheaton College historian[8] who years later would issue a charge in the form of a halting historical argument that Christians now do, but (in Charles Malik's words) "cannot afford to keep on living on the periphery of responsible intellectual existence."[9] In his widely discussed 1994 book, *The Scandal of the Evangelical Mind*, Noll laments that "the scandal of the evangelical mind is that there is not much of an evangelical mind."[10] And the scandal is none other than a failure to exercise the mind for Christ in all areas of life—nature, society, and art. Modern evangelicals, while enjoying dynamic success at a popular level, "have largely abandoned the universities, the arts, and other realms of 'high' culture."[11] Noll argued that as the Western university goes, so goes Western culture, including its spiritual heritage: "the great institutions of higher learning in Western culture function as the *mind* of Western culture."[12] Noll offered, like Malik before him, a call to integrity for the Christian in general and especially the Christian scholar.

---

7. Ibid., 312.
8. Since the fall 2006, Noll has been the Francis A. McAnaney Professor of History at the University of Notre Dame; he replaced now retired historian George Marsden.
9. See page 64 in chapter 2.
10. Mark Noll, *The Scandal of the Evangelical Mind* (Grand Rapids: Eerdmans, 1994), 1. Noll calls his book "a historical footnote in support of Malik's sage words [contained in his Two Tasks message]," 27.
11. Ibid., 3.
12. Ibid., 51. This theme will be picked up and discussed by Habib Malik in chapter 3.

One final work that has served as a rallying point for Christian scholars since Malik is George Marsden's *The Outrageous Idea of Christian Scholarship*.[13] The idea, outrageous to both secular and religious scholars, is that faith and learning are compatible. But Marsden argues that this outrageous idea is true—the fully integrated life *is* possible even for a Christian scholar. Still, Marsden is puzzled and asks, why "among so many academics who are professing Christians, all but a tiny minority keep quiet about the intellectual implications of their faith?"[14] Marsden's book is important because in it he attempts to spell out what Christian scholarship could look like in a pluralistic secular academy. His contention is that faith can and does make a positive contribution to learning, and it should therefore be granted a legitimate place in the market of ideas. Voluntary silence by religious scholars is not necessary in secular academia.

Malik's 1980 charge to live an integrated life within academia has been taken up (directly or indirectly) by many Christians. Plantinga, Noll, and Marsden are all examples of leading scholars within their academic field. *Time* magazine even named Noll one of America's twenty-five most influential evangelicals in 2005,[15] and his book, *America's God: From Jonathan Edwards to Abraham Lincoln*, was named "the most significant work of American historical scholarship" in 2002 by the *Atlantic Monthly*.[16] In this milieu set by those like Plantinga, Noll, and Marsden, there have been many encouraging highlights of God moving within academia—redeeming souls and redeeming the mind of individuals and the university in general. Those highlights include:

- A transformation taking place within the discipline of philosophy, which William Lane Craig discusses in chapter 8. This transformation is so alarming that one atheistic philosopher, Quentin Smith, laments "God is not 'dead' in academia; he returned to life in the late 1960s [beginning with Plantinga's influential book *God and Other Minds* in 1967] and is now alive and well in his last academic stronghold, philosophy

13. George Marsden, *The Outrageous Idea of Christian Scholarship* (Oxford: Oxford University Press, 1997).

14. Ibid., 6.

15. "The 25 Most Influential Evangelicals in America," *Time*, February 7, 2005, 42.

16. Books and Critics, *Atlantic Monthly*, December, 2002, 126.

departments."[17] This movement of God is evident in the
growth and vitality of Christian philosophy societies. For
example, the Society of Christian Philosophers, founded in
part by Plantinga in 1978, now includes over one thousand
members, a leading academic journal *Faith and Philosophy*,
and outreach programs to secular philosophy departments
in Russia and China.[18] The Evangelical Philosophy Society,
founded in 1974, has also experienced tremendous growth
in the last twenty-five years with around eight hundred
members, its own leading philosophy journal, *Philosophia
Christi*, and annual outreach events in the form of apologetic
conferences for lay people within the church. Further, Talbot School of Theology, led by philosophers J. P. Moreland,
William Lane Craig, and others, boasts the largest graduate
philosophy program in the world, sending its graduated
MA students into top PhD programs (over ninety students
to date) including Notre Dame, the University of Texas,
Oxford University, the University of Southern California,
and many others.[19] God is raising up a new generation of
Christian philosophers who, like Plantinga, are not content
to simply operate under the facile rules stipulated by secularism—instead these philosophers are embracing Malik's
charge to redeem the soul and redeem the mind.

• A growing para-university movement of Christian study
centers that exist alongside universities as a presence and
voice for Christ within secular academia. The explicit goal
of these Christian study centers is to help restore the plausibility of the Christian worldview by influencing professors
and students. In all of these study centers, Christian scholars
play an integral role in the founding, shaping, and direction

17. Quentin Smith, "The Metaphilosophy of Naturalism," *Philo* 4, no. 2
(2001): 4.
18. For a discussion of the founding of the Society of Christian Philosophers
see Kelly James Clark, "Introduction: The Literature of Confession," in *Philosophers Who Believe*, ed. Kelly James Clark (Downers Grove, IL: InterVarsity,
1993), 7–21.
19. This author numbers himself among those privileged to study philosophy
at Talbot, and is now in a leading secular PhD program. For more on how God is
using Talbot School of Theology (part of Biola University) in making inroads into
the larger philosophical world, see Agnieszka Tennant, "Masters of Philosophy,"
Christianity Today, June 2003, 46–48.

of the ministry. In additional to the well-established Center for Christian Studies (University of Virginia, 1976), a number of significant new Christian study centers over the last twenty-five years have developed, most within the last ten years: for instance, the MacLaurin Institute (University of Minnesota, 1982), the Centers for Christian Studies, International (University of Colorado at Boulder, Fort Collins, and Colorado Springs, 1983), the Christian Study Center of Gainesville (University of Florida–Gainesville, 2000), Chesterton House (Cornell University, 2000), the Rivendell Institute (Yale University, mid-1990s), and the John Newton International Center for Christian Studies (academic communities of central Pennsylvania, 2003), among others.

• A growing commitment by para-church organizations to engage and reach out to university professors. Faculty Commons (Campus Crusade for Christ's faculty ministry) and InterVarsity's Faculty Ministry were both founded in the last thirty years (1980 and 1975, respectively) in order to effectively minister to and with university professors. For example, a sub-ministry of Faculty Commons called Academic Initiative targets the ideas propagated within secular academia with an eye toward helping current and future professors integrate their faith with their scholarship. InterVarsity's Emerging Scholars Network boasts approximately three thousand members and is working to (among other things) establish mentoring relationships between senior Christian scholars and junior Christian scholars. Additionally, the International Institute for Christian Studies, founded in 1986, sends Christian professors into secular universities in countries outside North America so that someday every university student and professor in the world will have a chance to hear and consider the message of Christ from a faithful follower of Christ.

• Christian scholarly societies are flourishing. For a partial list see the "Connecting" site at FacultyLinc.com. Often these Christian scholarly societies hold annual conferences in conjunction with their secular counterpart, which provides opportunities for Christian scholars to network with

Christians from other institutions as well as to interact with other peers in their discipline.

• A general highlight: there is an increased commitment to the life of the mind and the influence of culture for Christ over the long-term. A few examples are: (1) The Harvey Fellows program, begun in 1992 as a program of the Mustard Seed Foundation, provides significant financial (around $15,000 per year) and relational support to outstanding Christian graduate students at our nation's top academic programs. The goal is to raise up a future generation of professors who are capable of doing first-rate academic work and who are faithful to Christ. To date, there are over two hundred Harvey Fellows worldwide representing forty academic fields and over $4 million in scholarship funds to Christian graduate students. (2) Christian worldview ministries with substantial involvement from university professors provide a platform for greater impact as well as a model for Christian witness in the university; examples include the Wilberforce Forum (a ministry of Prison Fellowship), the C. S. Lewis Foundation's Faculty Forum initiative (launched 1999) and the Veritas Forum (founded 1992 at Harvard).[20]

These highlights are just a few of the many encouraging events and happenings taking place today within academia by Christians and Christian scholars. Undoubtedly, the list could go on, citing numerous exemplary individuals and individual works, as well as the vast amount of work that is being done by Christian colleges and universities.[21] But this listing should suffice for my general

---

20. For an account of how the Veritas Forum began, see Kelly Monroe Kullberg, *Finding God Beyond Harvard: The Quest for Veritas* (Downers Grove, IL: InterVarsity, 2006).

21. To sight just a few highlights, consider (1) the Baylor University's 2012 plan, in which Baylor University seeks to establish itself as a premier and explicitly protestant Christian research university comparable with other first-rate research universities such as Princeton, Harvard, Yale, and the University of Chicago; (2) the Council for Christian Colleges and Universities (CCCU), an international higher education association of intentionally Christian colleges and universities, which has grown from thirty-eight members in 1976 to 105 members in North America and seventy-five affiliate members in twenty-four countries by 2006; and (3) high quality explicitly and implicitly Christian research published in leading academic journals and books as well as a reputable interdisciplinary journal, *Christian*

point: there are many things to be encouraged by, given the state of Christian scholarship and the Christian scholar since Charles Malik's call; God hasn't given up on us, nor has he given up on academia. But, as Habib Malik discusses in chapter 3, in every day and age new challenges face the believer—and this is no different for the Christian scholar today in the secular academia.

Distinctly religious viewpoints are not always welcome in academia. Arguably, the dominant ethos within scientific disciplines today is *scientism* (roughly, all we can know is what science tells us) and its close relative *naturalism* (roughly, all that exists is what science tells us exists). In the humanities, the dominant ethos is some version of postmodern *deconstructionism* (roughly, the idea that meaning within a "text" is a mercurial thing, impossible to pin down) and *relativism* (roughly, truth varies in relation to individuals, cultures, or conceptual schemes). Within this setting, Christianity is sometimes just ignored as irrelevant to intellectual discourse, and sometimes directly attacked. Here are a few recent examples:

- Since 9/11 there has been a new wave of assaults on religious belief by atheists, led by university professors and scholars. Books such as Richard Dawkins's *The God Delusion* (2006), Daniel Dennett's *Breaking the Spell: Religion as a Natural Phenomenon* (2006), and Sam Harris's *The End of Faith* (2004) and *Letter to a Christian Nation* (2006) have been selling by the thousands and have received much attention in the press and on college campuses.[22] The basic message of this wave of "new atheists" is that religion is not only silly—it is down-right dangerous.[23]
- There is often an unwillingness to even consider arguments or evidence contrary to the reigning evolutionary story in

---

Scholars Review. For more on the renaissance in Christian higher education see Michael Hamilton, "A Higher Education," *Christianity Today*, June 2005, 30–35.

22. Dawkins is the Charles Simonyi Professor of the Public Understanding of Science at Oxford University; Dennett is the B. Fletcher Professor of Philosophy at Tufts University; Harris is a PhD candidate in neuroscience at an undisclosed university.

23. For more on this new wave of atheism, see Jerry Adler, "The New Naysayers," *Newsweek*, September 11, 2006, 47–49. But these examples can be interpreted in more than one way. Recently, Richard Shweder, a professor of comparative human development at the University of Chicago, argued that these books by Dawkins, Dennett, and Harris reveal that "the armies of disbelief have been

the sciences. An example of this is the uproar that has been generated against a prominent researcher, Richard Stern-berg, at the Smithsonian's National Museum of Natural History after he published a peer-reviewed article by a leading proponent of intelligent design.[24] Sternberg was locked out of his office, shunned by colleagues, and accused of being a religious fundamentalist for having the audacity to accept an article critical of the established view of evolutionary theory. The point here isn't to call into question the validity of evolution (which I am happy to do); rather the point is to highlight the almost vitriolic reaction directed toward Sternberg (and others) for allowing a view that has been stigmatized as "religiously motivated" to gain a hearing in a mainstream academic journal.[25]

• This strong prejudice against explicit religious perspectives in mainstream academia arises within the humanities as well. Under the mantra of multiculturalism and diversity, Christianity and Christian viewpoints are often labeled as oppressive and imperialistic. In a pluralistic world, any call to openly Christian scholarship is often viewed with

provoked." Atheism has gone from an advancing movement to being on the defensive, all in the period of one generation. Perhaps, Shweder wonders, "the popularity of the current counterattack on religion cloaks a renewed and intense anxiety within secular society that it is not the story of religion but rather the story of the Enlightenment that may be more illusory than real." Minimally at least, what these examples reveal is, for Christian academics, there can be no neutral ground, no opting-out from this debate. See Richard Shweder, op-ed, "Atheists Agonistes," *New York Times*, November 27, 2006.

24. The article is by Stephen Meyer, "The Origin of Biological Information and the Higher Taxonomic Categories," *Proceedings of the Biological Society of Washington* 117 (2004): 213–39. Even more recently, astronomer Guillermo Gonzalez, whose book *The Privileged Planet* is discussed by Robert Kaita in chapter 6, was denied tenure at Iowa State University; Gonzalez claims that the reason is because he is a proponent of intelligent design. See Geoff Brumfiel, "Darwin Sceptic Says View Cost Tenure," *Nature*, 447 (May 24, 2007): 364. In this article, Robert Park, a physicist at the University of Maryland, states regarding Gonzalez, "Anyone who believes that an intelligent force set the Earth's location doesn't understand probability's role in the Universe. . . . Such a person is hardly qualified to teach others about the scientific method." All this is despite the fact that Gozalez has distinguished himself as a stellar scholar.

25. For more, see Joyce Howard Price, "Researcher Claims Bias by Smithsonian," *Washington Times*, February, 13, 2005.

suspicion by many minority groups who have suffered discrimination in the past, such as gays and lesbians, Marxists scholars, feminist scholars, and even advocates of sheer secularism.[26]

- Recent studies indicate that while American professors are more religious than is typically assumed, it is clear that on the whole, professors are less religious than the general U.S. population, and the more elite the school, the less religious the professorate.[27] This result places a damper on some of the highlights mentioned above, for it suggests that much more needs to be done at just those places where much of the intellectual and cultural capital is generated in society (i.e., the elite schools). Another disturbing trend concerns professors' views on the Bible. While roughly 18 percent of the general U.S. population believes the Bible is "an ancient book of fables, legends, history, and moral precepts," almost 52 percent of professors in general, and 73 percent of those professors teaching in elite universities, hold the "ancient book of fables" view.[28] With this attitude toward the Bible, it is easy to see how Christian scholars functioning in such a setting can easily begin to neglect the reading and internalizing of Scripture. Couple this temptation with the reality of over-specialization and the result is often, as William Lane Craig discusses in chapter 8, a Christian professorate with barely a "Sunday school" knowledge of Scripture and theology.

As before, lowlights could be multiplied, but the general point should be clear: academia is not always welcome or open to the religious point of view. The dominant secular ethos operates as a powerful control over what is or is not acceptable as public knowledge, often

---

26. For more on this, see Marsden, *Outrageous Idea of Christian Scholarship*, 25–43.

27. For a summary of the report, see Thomas Bartlett, "Professors Are More Religious Than Some Might Assume, Survey Finds," *The Chronicle of Higher Education*, October 20, 2006, A26. For the full report, see http://www.wjh.harvard.edu/soc/faculty/gross/religions.pdf.

28. Conversely, 80 percent of the general population believes that the Bible is either the "actual word of God or the inspired word of God," whereas only 48 percent of professors hold this view, with the percentage significantly decreasing the more elite the school.

resulting in the marginalization of or outright attack on Christianity (or religion in general).

But sometimes the challenges the Christian scholar faces are subtler. For example, I once heard a Christian professor describe to a group of Christian graduate students the reality of graduate school as a kind of boot camp. The constant grind of the university conforms its "cadets" into its own image. From first-year graduate students to ABD doctoral candidates, the university curriculum, ethos, and pace leave little room for attention to character, spiritual well-being, and integrative thinking. The name of the academic game is to successfully navigate the degree process: finish coursework, learn a foreign language, conduct original research, be a good TA, grade hundreds of undergraduate exams and homework assignments, teach introductory sections within the discipline, present at a few conferences, get published if lucky, and all the while, live on a paltry stipend. Any attention to the soul or integrative thinking in such an environment is extracurricular. Given this lack of margin, it is easy to place any of these ancillary matters toward the side, perhaps promising to oneself that these matters will be picked up again when things are not so busy.

Of course, the reality is that things only get busier. As Peter Kreeft discusses in chapter 4, one of the characteristics of the modern university is that everyone is in a hurry. Any future promises to devote more time and energy to thinking Christianly about one's discipline or to giving more attention to one's own soul or the souls of others are pushed further away as the goal of a PhD is supplanted with the new goal of making tenure. Often, somewhere along this process, it seems that the fire for Christ that once burned bright as a new PhD student has dimmed, views have been formed without attention or assistance from the Spirit, and a sense of calling from God has ceased to be heard. *Perhaps* something like this has been taking place within secular academia among some of the professors who are Christians; I am not sure. But what does seem clear is this: often the biggest obstacle to making a difference for Christ within academia does not have to do with the threat from without. Rather, if I may speak bluntly and of myself as well, the threat is *us*—our own heart or mind is not captivated with the love of Christ. It has been said that our lives are shaped by what we think great. Perhaps we need a renewed vision of the greatness of Christ to counter the pull of the university, which often, unbeknownst to us, has conformed us into its own image in pursuit of its own greatness.

Transforming the mind of the university so that it can be a place where Christianity is understood as a legitimate option will take much time and require a great deal of patience. But the transformation will take place only through transformed people. For as C. S. Lewis observed,

> this very obvious fact—that each generation is taught by an earlier generation—must be kept very firmly in mind. . . . None can give to another what he does not possess himself. No generation can bequeath to its successor what it has not got. You may frame the syllabus as you please. But when you have planned and reported *ad nauseam*, if we are skeptical we shall teach only skepticism to our pupils, if fools only folly, if vulgar only vulgarity, if saints sanctity, if heroes heroism. . . . Nothing which was not in the teachers can flow from them into the pupils. We shall all admit that a man who knows no Greek himself cannot teach Greek to his form: but it is equally certain that a man whose mind was formed in a period of cynicism and disillusion, cannot teach hope and fortitude.[29]

If we are to teach Christ in words and action, we must be Christ to our students and colleagues. And in order to be Christ, we must understand who Christ is and what he is doing in redemptive history. And that means we must view Scripture as more than simply fable. Rather, it must be understood as our lifeline, the story that gives our lives context and meaning—and the story that gives our scholarship context and meaning as well.

The Metanarrative of Scripture and Its Implications for the Christian Scholar

My purpose is to look at the task of integration from the vantage of Christianity that aims to be faithful to Scripture. Today, in the postmodern culture in which we find ourselves, there is, in the words

---

29. C. S. Lewis, "On the Transmission of Christianity," in *God in the Dock: Essays on Theology and Ethics,* ed. Walter Hooper (Grand Rapids: Eerdmans, 1970), 116.

of Jean-Francois Lyotard, an "incredulity toward metanarrative(s)."[30]
Yet, a most natural reading of Scripture reveals the fact that the
Bible is a metanarrative: an overarching story that explains (or
captures) all of reality. The Bible introduces characters (e.g., God,
angels, man), scenes (heaven, earth, etc.), and a plotline (creation,
fall, redemption, and restoration). Thus, the Bible reads like a good
story. However, it is more than a good story—in it we find revealed
truth about God, self, and the world. In order to properly understand
concepts that traditionally belong to systematic theology such as
anthropology, Christology, or ecclesiology, it is important to grasp the
overall metanarrative of Scripture. For example, it makes no sense to
say to someone, "you need to be redeemed," unless he has a concept
of what exactly he needs to be "redeemed" from. Additionally, it
makes no sense to say, "Christians ought to integrate their faith with
their scholarship" unless there is an understanding of the *purpose*
and *mission* of the Christian life in general. In this section, I shall
provide a brief outline of the major plotline of Scripture. In doing
so, I will identify major characters in the story as well as important
themes that inform the scholarly enterprise.

The first scene in the biblical story is *creation*. The God who is
there (to borrow a phrase from Francis Schaeffer) is a God who
acts. He speaks and his creation comes into being. Early on we see
that God creates humans as his pinnacle of creation. Humans are
created in the image of God (Gen. 1:26–27), and thus are endowed
with great dignity and value. So, in Genesis 1, God creates the
first home for human persons and then gives them a purpose. The
purpose found in Genesis 1:28 is twofold: (1) to protect what has
been given, and (2) to extend the glory of God to the ends of the
earth. Note, this purpose is tied to the fact that humans are made
in the image of God. We are to be fruitful and multiply not because
God is interested in numbers, but because as image bearers we can
extend the image of God to all of creation. Furthermore, with the
creation of the first couple (Genesis 2), we see a picture of how
things are supposed to be: intimacy with God and harmony with
each other. The Hebrew word for this universal state of flourishing
is *shalom*.

---

30. Jean-Francois Lyotard, *The Postmodern Condition: A Report on Knowledge*
(Minneapolis: University of Minnesota Press, 1984), xxiv.

Creation and the Task of Integration

Three themes related to the creation account are relevant to the task of integration. First, the fact that *God created the universe, while he himself is uncreated* establishes a particular relationship between God and the universe.[31] The initial five words in the Bible shape everything for the Christian scholar: "In the beginning God created . . ." (Gen. 1:1). The central origin account of the secular academy, shaped by scientific naturalism, is antithetical to the biblical prolegomenon: "In the beginning matter. . . ." As Francis Schaeffer argues, "Everything goes back to the beginning and thus the system has a unique beauty and perfection because everything is under the apex of the system. Everything begins with the kind of God who is 'there.' This is the beginning and apex of the whole, and everything flows from this in a non-contradictory way."[32] In his book, *Truth to Tell*, Lesslie Newbigin laments the fact that our culture, as heir of Descartes, starts in the wrong place by elevating the human knower, instead of God, as the starting point in the search for certainty.[33] Newbigin writes, "We have to offer a new starting point for thought. That starting point is God's revelation of his being and purpose in those events which form the substance of the Scriptures and which have their center and determining focus in the events concerning Jesus."[34] This world, created by God, is a world that is moving in a certain direction. There is teleology in the world. History is linear, it is going somewhere; it has an ending. Furthermore, since God exists sans creation and brought all things

31. D. A. Carson, *The Gagging of God* (Grand Rapids: Zondervan, 1996), 201–2.

32. Francis A. Schaeffer, *Escape from Reason* (Downers Grove, IL: InterVarsity, 1968), 25.

33. Lesslie Newbigin, *Truth to Tell: The Gospel as Public Truth* (Grand Rapids: Eerdmans, 1991), 26–28. Of course we can only actually begin with our own epistemic situation, and not God's. Rather, the point is that God is no longer seen as the *ground* of our knowledge in this post-Cartesian world. God has created man as *knowing* creatures, and this theological grounding provides justification for how it is that human subjects can have knowledge about the objective world. Alvin Plantinga has argued this point in his own way, stating that warrant (i.e., that which in addition to true belief is necessary for knowledge) supervenes on among other things, a properly functioning cognitive faculty operating according to a design plan. See Alvin Plantinga, *Warrant and Proper Function* (New York: Oxford University Press, 1993).

34. Ibid., 28.

into existence out of nothing (*creatio ex nihilo*), it follows that there is a particular "givenness" to things that the scholar must come to terms with. Contrary to the postmodern critique, there is a reality outside of the human person, and the human being finds himself in a world that is not of his own making. Thus, humans do not have pride of place in matters of ontology or epistemology. God is infinite, everything else is finite; everything else is creature.

Second, *God is for human flourishing*. As originally created, all that God made was good (Gen. 1:4, 10, 12, 18, 21, 25) and in the case of human beings, "very good" (Gen. 1:31). We didn't come into the world flawed; rather, we came into the world whole. The biblical term for the wholeness God intends humans to experience is *shalom*. As theologian Cornelius Plantinga states, "Shalom *means universal flourishing, wholeness, and delight*—a rich state of affairs in which natural needs are satisfied and natural gifts fruitfully employed, a state of affairs that inspires joyful wonder as its Creator and Savior open doors and welcomes the creatures in whom he delights."[35] When humans enter a state of *shalom*, they function in the way God intended them to function, and God is glorified. Thus, Aristotle's *eudaimonia* finds its fullest expression in the Christian vision of human dignity and happiness. Humans, created in the image of God, are meant to flourish in light of their nature—in intimacy with God and harmony with each other and the created order.

Third, *as image bearers, humans are accountable to God*.[36] As free personal agents made in the image of God, humans are given a unique place in the created order: our actions have consequences. This fact is essential to understanding the biblical plotline. We were not only made *by* God but *for* him. Failure to live acknowledging our dependence and accountability toward God leads to the deepest anarchy. It is here, as D. A. Carson points out, that the loss of a Christian worldview is most felt. Academia, and American culture in general, does not want to be accountable to anyone. Darwinism teaches us that we are determined. There is no longer any such thing as culpable sin. Rather, we are all victims. Crime is attributed to genetics and environment instead of moral indiscretion. The biblical account is clear, however: humans, created in the image of God are

---

35. Cornelius Plantinga Jr., *Not the Way It's Supposed to Be: A Breviary of Sin* (Grand Rapids: Eerdmans, 1995), 10. Yes, this is Alvin Plantinga's brother.
36. Carson, *The Gagging of God*, 206–9.

accountable for their actions. As scene 2 opens within the plotline of Scripture, this truth becomes all too clear.

Scene 2 within the biblical story is the *fall of humanity*. As Genesis 3 opens, the central question facing the first couple is, will they fulfill the purpose for which they are made? The answer, as is well known, is no. The immediate effect of Adam and Eve's disobedience is a loss of *shalom*; things are no longer the way they are supposed to be. Alienation, shame, and guilt are experienced instead of intimacy and loving presence. Humanity is kicked out of their "*shalomic* home," and must forge ahead in a cold and cruel world.[37] Due to the "original sin" of this first couple, all of humanity will be born into the world in a state of alienation (between God and each other) and disharmony. There are at least two implications for integration by the Christian scholar related to the fall of humanity. First, *since the Enlightenment, the autonomous man tends to minimize or dismiss sin*.[38] With the rise of Rousseau (and later Freud), the view that many of humanity's problems arise from frustrations caused by civilization's moral proclivities has become entrenched. Works from cultural anthropologists such as Margaret Mead's *Coming of Age in Samoa*[39] have supposedly confirmed the Freudian premise that apart from cultural mores there are no innate moral inhibitions. If, as Bertrand Russell argued in 1903, man is just a "collocation of atoms" in which "no fire, no heroism, no intensity of thought and feeling, can preserve an individual life beyond the grave," then sin makes no sense.[40] As Cornelius Plantinga has pointed out, "We can understand neither shalom nor sin apart from reference to God."[41] Sin is ultimately an affront against God. This leads to the second implication of the fall: *for the Christian scholar, a biblical view of sin and the human dilemma is essential in order to prescribe the correct solution*. If sin is gone, then what need is there for a

---

37. Hence, Cornelius Plantinga calls sin "culpable shalom-breaking." C. Plantinga, *Not the Way It's Supposed to Be*, 14.

38. Carson, *The Gagging of God*, 216–17.

39. Margaret Mead, *Coming of Age in Samoa: A Psychological Study of Primitive Youth for Western Civilization* (New York: Wm. Morrow, 1967), as cited in Carson, *The Gagging of God*, 217.

40. Bertrand Russell, "A Free Man's Worship," in *Why I Am Not a Christian* (New York: Simon & Schuster, 1957), 107.

41. C. Plantinga, *Not the Way It's Supposed to Be*, 12–18.

Savior? The trend within liberal Christianity to limit the human condition to terms of social justice only, distorts the central message of the gospel. According to Scripture, the central need for humans is redemption from the consequences of sin: something has gone wrong, *shalom* has been destroyed. Thus, while humans live in a state of alienation from God resulting from the fall, they still are created in the image of God (marred as it may be). The effect of sin includes all aspects of humanity: volitional, intellectual, and emotional. However, embedded within the creation account is the truth that God provides for his own: the stage has been set for God's rescue mission.[42]

Scene 3 of the biblical story opens with the *coming of Christ*. In the incarnation, Christ comes to earth "in the flesh," forever removing the unbridgeable dichotomy between the spiritual and natural world. The birth narratives (Matthew 1–2; Luke 1–2) bring together two different orders: God and human beings. The desperate plight begun in Eden now finds solution in Jesus: the opening chapter of the New Testament declares that he will save his people from their sins (Matt. 1:21). The prophetic anticipation of a Messiah and the promise given to Abraham (Gen. 12:1–3) find their fruition in the coming of Jesus. He is the solution to evil and the guilt of sin. Furthermore, the rush of the narrative in each of the gospels is toward the cross. Jesus came to die, to redeem humanity, and "to seek and to save what was lost" (Luke 19:10). Thus, in Jesus we find the reestablishment of the originally intended divine order; humans can once again flourish in intimacy with God and harmony with each other and the created world, fulfilling the *shalomic* vision as God's vice-regents. Jesus inaugurates the kingdom and one day he will consummate it.[43] God the Father sent his Son on a rescue mission. As the gospel narratives close, and Jesus returns to the Father, he gives a final command: his followers are to be involved in outreach to the entire world (Matt. 28:19–20). Thus, the New

---

42. As Carson points out, God generously provided for his image bearers in the garden. Even after the ravages of sin, God provided clothes for Adam and Eve (Gen. 3:21), showing his continued love and care of his people. Carson, *The Gagging of God*, 234.

43. Carson writes, "Thus the kingdom, viewed as that subset of the reign of God under which there is life, can be understood to be a bringing back into history of the final kingdom of blessedness that still awaits." Carson, *The Gagging of God*, 262.

Testament documents pulsate with a living tension between the "already" and the "not yet." The kingdom has already come in Jesus, but it is not yet here in its consummation. Within this tension, we find the mission of the church to the nations: "this gospel of the kingdom will be preached in the whole world as a testimony to all nations, and then the end will come" (Matt. 24:14).

The Person of Christ and the Task of Integration

There are four implications related to the person of Christ and the task of integration. First, *with the incarnation we see that the supernatural and the natural realms are not closed off to each other*.[44] While God is the transcendent Creator of the universe, he is also immanent within his creation. God is present and active within history and nature. The supernatural can be known because we live in a spiritually "open" universe. Marsden states, "Acceptance of the incarnation, however, seems to presuppose that we can know about the transcendent through ordinary contingent means such as the testimony of others and evidence drawn from our own experience."[45]

Second, in God's progressive revelation, *we learn that God created the world through the divine agent of the Logos* (John 1:1–3). Christ, the second member of the Trinity, is the divine Logos. The Logos is the agent of creation for both the human and nonhuman world (see also 1 Cor. 8:6; Col. 1:16–17; Heb. 1:3). Furthermore, we learn in Colossians 2:3 that in Jesus are hidden "all the treasures of wisdom and knowledge." Thus, the world is intelligible because it is created by intelligence. Jesus, as the divine Logos, imparts information to us. The philosopher and scientist William Dembski states, "Information—the information that God speaks to create the world, the information that continually proceeds from God in sustaining the world and acting in it and the information that passes between God's creatures—this is the bridge that connects transcendence and immanence. All of this information is mediated through the divine Logos, who is before all things and in whom all things consist (Col. 1:17)."[46] For the Christian scholar, Jesus must

---

44. Marsden, *Outrageous Idea of Christian Scholarship*, 90.
45. Ibid.
46. William Dembski, *Intelligent Design* (Downers Grove, IL: InterVarsity, 1999), 233.

be viewed for who he is—the smartest person ever. Jesus possesses intellectual virtue to speak on all matters of reality.[47] A large part of the anti-intellectualism that evangelicalism suffers from is due to a truncated view of the person of Jesus. Jesus is often taken to possess spiritual or moral authority to speak into a person's life, but when it comes to matters of reality, Jesus is not often thought of as a reliable source of authority. Thus, while Jesus isn't a scientist per se, making pronouncements on quarks or relativity theory, the Christian scholar needs to acknowledge Jesus as the source for the very possibility of science itself. The possibility of scholarship, Christian or otherwise, is due to the fact that the divine Logos speaks, and information is imparted into all of reality. As Christian scholars, this truth should cause us to courageously advance a Christian view of reality within academia.

Third, *at the heart of God's redemptive purpose is the renewing of the human mind.*[48] Scripture repeatedly speaks of the non-Christian mind as futile and hostile to God (e.g., Rom. 8:7; Eph. 4:17–24; Col. 1:21). For the redeemed person, there is a radical change in one's orientation, and this radical change includes the life of the mind. One of the greatest passages ever penned on spiritual formation by Paul, Romans 12:1–2, puts the mind front and center in the process of transformation unto Christ. Christians are to "be transformed" by the "renewing of their minds," and ultimately this redemption of the mind results from the gospel.

This leads me to the last implication for the Christian scholar: *Jesus' mission must be the Christian scholar's mission.* Jesus came "to seek and to save what was lost" (Luke 19:10). Furthermore, he entrusted this mission to his followers before he ascended to heaven (Matt. 28:19–20). Therefore, any view of scholarship that leaves out this missional aspect loses sight of the overall purpose to our work.

---

47. For helpful discussions on the topic of Jesus as being smart, see Dallas Willard, *The Divine Conspiracy* (San Francisco: HarperCollins, 1998), 61–95; Douglas Groothuis, *On Jesus* (Belmont, CA: Wadsworth, 2003), 23–35; and Dallas Willard, "Jesus, the Logician," *Christian Scholars Review* XXVIII, no. 4 (1999): 605–14. Groothuis's work does a good job of demonstrating Jesus' use of reason and argumentation. Passages such as Matthew 22:15–33, Luke 2:41–52, and many others reveal the fact that the incarnate Jesus, out of his *human* nature, and not just as the eternal, divine Logos, possessed the highest intellectual virtue.

48. See Brad Green, "Theological and Philosophical Foundations," in *Shaping a Christian Worldview,* eds. David Dockery and Gregory Alan Thornbury (Nashville: Broadman, 2002), 68–73.

The philosopher Greg Ganssle states, "It is not enough to integrate Christian *beliefs* with our research, we must integrate all that God calls us to in terms of his redemptive Christian *mission* with all we do as scholars and teachers."[49] Any definition of integration which leaves out the mission of Christ as it relates to the scholar's work and life will ultimately be unhelpful.[50]

The fourth scene in the plotline of Scripture is *the coming of the Spirit*. As heirs of the new covenant, Christians have been given a deposit in the form of the third person of the triune God (Eph. 1:13–14). It is the Holy Spirit who enables people to understand and know the truth of the gospel (1 Cor. 2:14). The Spirit convicts people of their sins (John 16:7–11) and is a helper and guide for the Christian (John 14:16). For the purposes of integration, it is important to keep in mind that it is the Spirit who enables the Christian to exercise faith in God. While the "content" of the faith (i.e., the knowledge claims) are available to all, only God can bring about "saving faith" for those he chooses to draw to himself (John 6:37).[51]

The climax of the biblical plotline is the *renewal of all things as Christ reconciles everything to himself at the end of the age*. The climactic vision of the Bible found in Revelation 21 and 22 pulls together all the plotline and sub-themes found in both the Old and New Testaments. All things are renewed/reconciled in Christ (Col. 1:19–20). There is a new heaven and new earth (2 Peter 3:13). Mankind will experience perfect intimacy with God and each other (Rev. 21:3–4) and will worship God and the lamb for eternity

---

49. Gregory Ganssle, "The Next Breakthrough in Christian Scholarship," unpublished paper delivered at the National Faculty Leadership Conference, Washington, DC on June 25, 2004.

50. I will deal more with the issue of mission more fully below. For now, let me be clear that the redemptive responsibility of the Christian scholar is holistic, integrated, and interdependent, not oversimplified, propositional proselytizing.

51. I am not making a theological claim regarding the relationship between human freedom and God's sovereignty in relation to saving faith. Whether one holds to a libertarian view of human freedom or a compatibilist view of human freedom, the biblical truth remains the same: it is God's Spirit that enlivens a spiritually "dead" person. Whether the human agent plays any role (apart from passive recipient of God's grace) in saving faith is not necessary to address here. The point is that the Spirit must regenerate a person in order to transfer him from the kingdom of darkness into the kingdom of light.

(Revelation 5). In a word, *shalom* will be fully restored. Things will once again be as they should be.

This discussion does not simply constitute an exercise in theological "throat-clearing." Rather, the point of reviewing the biblical story is that it has a point. History is going somewhere—there is a purpose! As Christian scholars, our scholarly work and life need to take place within the context of this great drama. Without the context of the metanarrative of Scripture, the Christian scholar runs the risk of compartmentalizing his scholarly work and life from his personal piety. However, as should now be clear, the biblical plotline has many implications for the integration of the two tasks into the scholarly life. These implications include not just the task of integrating our Christian beliefs within a specific discipline, but the task of integrating *all* God calls us to with *all* we do as scholars.

The Fully Integrated Life of the Christian Scholar Made More Concrete

As we have seen, then, Christianity is fundamentally about a person: Christ, the second person of the Trinity. But, Christianity is also a claim about reality—a reality created and sustained by Christ. As such, a Christian worldview includes propositions about the way the world is. A person and propositions, personal and abstract, the soul and the mind. More concretely, a fully integrated life for the Christian scholar in our day and age might look something like this:

> A Christian scholar is integrating his faith with his scholarship when he is engaged in either explicit Christian research or latent Christian research (the mind), while seeking God with all his being (the soul), which flows into worship of God and pursuit of people through his scholarly work and life (mission: redeeming the soul and mind).

This working definition of a fully-integrated life for the Christian scholar captures both an inward focus (the mind and soul of the Christian scholar) as well as an outward and upward focus (toward others and God). In the remainder of this section, I will attempt to unpack this working definition.

First, let's consider the implication of what I am proposing. What is the net result if Christians within academia begin to live integrated lives as prescribed above? In short, what are we after? A new Christian theocracy within the academy? A place at the table? Respectability? Marsden and others are rightly wary of a new establishment of Christian dominance.[52] I agree that within the pragmatic academy, pluralism is the best method for dealing peacefully and with equity among diverse people and belief systems.[53] Gone are the days of Constantinian Christianity where Christianity rules the culture. Rather, we should be *principled pluralists*—recognizing that to be a Christian is always to stand in tension with what the Bible calls the world.

But the pluralism we ought to subscribe to is not what Lesslie Newbigin calls "agnostic pluralism."[54] According to Newbigin, with agnostic pluralism, "we are free to have our own opinions provided we agree that they are only personal opinions."[55] This type of agnostic pluralism will only get Christians a seat at the table at the cost of making the table relative. The type of pluralism Christians should strive for within the secular academy and the net effect of employing the model of integration offered here is what Newbigin calls "committed pluralism."[56] With committed pluralism, the gospel message is proclaimed not as a system of honorable values, but as a truth that corresponds to reality. As such the proclamation of the gospel becomes part of the continuing conversation that shapes public doctrine. With committed pluralism, Newbigin states, "we can look for and work for a time when Christian leadership (not Christian domination) can shape society" and "shape the plausibility structure within which people make their decisions and come to their beliefs."[57]

This "transformational Christian vision,"[58] coupled with a sense of vocation, informs and motivates the scholarly enterprise for the Christian. But what does it mean to say one's scholarship is Christian? Does this mean it must employ theological or religious language

52. Marsden, *The Outrageous Idea of Christian Scholarship*, 13–24.
53. Ibid., 45–46.
54. Newbigin, *Truth to Tell*, 58–64.
55. Ibid., 59.
56. Ibid., 84–85.
57. Ibid., 85.
58. From C. Stephen Evans, "The Calling of the Christian Scholar-Teacher," in *Faithful Learning and the Christian Scholarly Vocation*, eds. Douglas Henry and Bob Agee (Grand Rapids: Eerdmans, 2003), 29.

at every turn? The short answer is "no." Some scholarship will be explicitly Christian.[59] In explicit Christian research, the scholar is asking a distinctly Christian question directly about the subject matter of the particular discipline (or view within) or applying distinctively Christian concepts to a particular problem or issue. The Christian scholar may find his discipline basically valid, yet lacking in certain ways when viewed from a Christian perspective. Many of the academic disciplines (or views within) have much in common with Christian faith, yet are lacking in its overall vision of truth. The Christian scholar, by correcting errors and supplementing narrow visions of truth from a Christian perspective, contributes to the transformation of the discipline.

But scholarship within the secular academy doesn't have to be explicitly Christian in order to count as faithful integration. One's Christianity can be, and often *will* be in applied disciplines, latent. By latent Christian research I (partly) mean what C. S. Lewis had in mind in his lecture to an assembly of Anglican priests and youth leaders in Wales during Easter, 1945:

> I believe that any Christian who is qualified to write a good popular book on any science may do much more by that than by any directly apologetic work. The difficulty we are up against is this. We can make people (often) attend to the Christian point of view for half an hour or so; but the moment they have gone away from our lecture or laid down our article, they are plunged back into a world where the opposite position is taken for granted. As long as that situation exists, widespread success is simply impossible. We must attack the enemy's line of communication. What we want is not more little books about Christianity, but more little books by Christians on other subjects—with their Christianity *latent*. You can see this most easily if you look at it the other way round. Our Faith is not very likely to be shaken by any book on Hinduism. But if whenever we read an

---

59. Following David Wolfe and Ronald Nelson, William Hasker provides a good discussion of the various integrative strategies, that is, the compatibilist, transformationalist, and reconstructionist strategies. In what follows, I shall loosely follow Hasker's terminology regarding the strategy of tranformational-ism. Thus, one of the primary questions asked by the scholar engaging in explicit Christian research seeking to transform a particular discipline (or aspect of the discipline) is, how does a distinctively Christian view of *x* transform the domi-nant view of *x* within the discipline (where *x* is, e.g., economic theory, human nature, reality, or whatever)? See William Hasker, "Faith-Learning Integration: An Overview," *Christian Scholars Review* XXI, no. 3, (March 1992): 231–48.

elementary book on Geology, Botany, Politics, or Astronomy, we found
that its implications were Hindu, that would shake us. It is not the
books written in direct defense of Materialism that make the modern
man a materialist; it is the materialistic assumptions in all the other
books. In the same way, it is not books on Christianity that will really
trouble him. But he would be troubled if, whenever he wanted a cheap
popular introduction to some science, the best work on the market
was always by a Christian.[60]

Thus, while the Christian scholar might not quote from the Bible
in his published research, his research is consistent with and/or
implies a robust Christian worldview. The philosopher Stephen
Evans provides a helpful distinction between two different types of
latent Christian research.[61] First, there is *purely vocational Christian
research* where, for example, a Christian mathematician constructs
the same mathematical proofs as a non-Christian, or a Christian
chemist performs the same experiment as a non-Christian, yet
the motive in the case of the Christian is to honor God by doing
the best scholarship one can. Doing excellent work, contributing
to the development of new knowledge, or demonstrating that it
is possible to be a thoughtful person and still be a Christian all
bear witness to the kingdom of God and qualify as latent Christian
research. Second, Evans discusses *implicit Christian research* (this
kind of latent Christian research is captured nicely in the C. S.
Lewis quote above) where, for example, the scholar attempts to
show something Christians know to be true without using overtly
Christian terms or concepts, or a particular research program or
hypothesis is motivated by Christian concerns without being overtly
Christian.[62]

---

60. Lewis, "Christian Apologetics," 93.
61. Stephen Evans, "The Calling of the Christian Scholar-Teacher," 34–36.
Evans also provides a useful "relevance continuum" to help make sense of the
ways in which academic content and the Christian faith are likely to be integrated
in various disciplines. For example, while issues pertaining to faith are relevant
to every discipline, they become more relevant as one moves from mathematics to the natural sciences, then to the human sciences, then to history, then to
literature and the arts, and finally to philosophy and theology. Ibid., 40.
62. It is sometimes a bit more difficult to determine if one's own research
or another's qualifies as latent Christian research (since it is not *overtly* so!).
The following might be helpful: in order to determine if the end product (i.e.,
published articles or books) of one's research or another's should be properly
categorized as latent Christian research, one of the following second-order

Whether a Christian scholar engages in explicit or latent Christian research is often a function of the intended audience. The more explicitly Christian, the more *visible* the faith dimension will be within a particular research program or end product. With latent Christian research, it is possible that the reader would be unaware of the imbedded Christian assumptions (such as the intelligibility of language, the uniformity of nature, the reality of an external world) within a particular work, and he would therefore need to begin to ask probing questions in order to tease out the specific worldview implications. Both types of Christian research are needed, and it is up to the particular scholars (ideally a group of scholars) within a discipline to formulate an appropriate strategy to begin transforming the discipline where necessary.

At this point a distinction should be made between *theoretical* and *applied* disciplines. While this distinction isn't clear-cut (applied disciplines have a theoretical basis and theoretical disciplines have some practical nature), it is still a significant factor when considering

---

questions must be affirmed when applied to a particular research program or end product: "Does *y* imply Christianity?" (to determine if the research qualifies for what Evans calls *implicit Christian research* or Lewis calls *latent Christian scholarship*); or "Is *y* consistent with Christianity?" (to determine if the research qualifies for what Evans calls *purely vocational Christian scholarship*), where *y* stands for a particular research program or end product. To ask second-order questions is to assume a vantage point one step removed from the particular research program or end product. Since the Christian assumptions are embedded within the research in this case, it is necessary to ask second-order questions about the research itself in order to determine if it qualifies as Christian research. Notice, this sets a natural boundary of acceptability for the Christian scholar. The thoughtful reader might ask at this point, "But, given this definition, wouldn't research conducted by many non-Christian scholars qualify as latent Christian research?" The answer, counterintuitively, seems to be a qualified "yes." However, as will be discussed further, even if the scholarship itself is consistent with Christianity or even implies Christianity, the integration of faith and scholarship for the scholar (Christian or otherwise) is not obtained. The *object* of the integrative task as defined above is the *person* (i.e., the career of the epistemic and moral agent) and not just his published work. For the non-Christian, an integrated life will fail to be obtained because the truths (or implications from the truths) produced from the latent Christian research are not fully integrated with the rest of his belief system. Furthermore, following the often cited aphorism "all truth is God's truth" as well as the fact that much of Western society still operates out of an inherited theistic framework, we would expect to find much truth within academia, even from non-Christian sources.

the various dimensions of integration. William Hasker succinctly states, "One discipline (i.e., theoretical) aims primarily at teaching its students to *know* something, the other (i.e., applied) at teaching them to *do* something."[63] As a general rule, the more applied the research, the more latent one's Christianity.[64] At the applied level, a mechanical engineer will (often) perform the same equations and utilize the same methods in his scholarly research whether or not he is a Christian. His Christianity will be latent—consistent with a Christian worldview, but not explicitly Christian. As the mechanical engineer explores the theoretical basis of his discipline, probing issues concerning epistemological or metaphysical "foundations" will become more pressing and ultimately more explicitly Christian. In other words, the foundations for the possibility of science, such as the uniformity of nature, the intelligibility of nature, etc., can be grounded only in a theistic worldview.

Perhaps an example of explicit and latent Christian scholarship is in order. Paul Moser's article, "Jesus and Philosophy: On the Questions We Ask,"[65] begins, "What if anything, has Jesus to do with philosophy?" Moser goes on to argue that Jesus as Lord means that he is Lord of our time, the research we engage in, and the very questions we ask. Furthermore, philosophy done under the authority of Jesus becomes agape-oriented ministry. Moser argues that faithful disciples of Jesus must transcend the discussion mode and move to the obedience mode of human discourse. Doing philosophy in the obedience mode means moving beyond mere questions to loving God and people in service to the mission of the church. Moser unabashedly brings all of the knowledge at his disposal, including Scripture, to bear as he asks the question, what does Jesus have to do with philosophy? Even given the Christian renaissance taking place in philosophy, Moser's answer to this question serves as an indictment of much of Christian philosophy as it is currently practiced (i.e., in the discussion mode only). Moser explicitly critiques the discipline of philosophy from the perspective

---

63. William Hasker, "Faith-Learning Integration," 239.

64. Of course this is only a general rule, and counter-examples are easy to come by. For example, the sub-discipline of applied ethics is highly theoretical—employing metaphysical truths to real-life situations. As such, one's Christian perspective might be more explicit than latent in this case.

65. Paul Moser, "Jesus and Philosophy: On the Questions We Ask," *Faith and Philosophy* 22, no. 3 (July 2005): 261–83.

of the person and mission of Jesus Christ. If taken seriously (and applied), Jesus as Lord will lead to the transformation of the scholar as well as the discipline as it moves from perpetual questioning to agape-oriented service.

The intelligent design movement can be identified as a latent Christian research program in the spirit of C. S. Lewis. Their critics notwithstanding, intelligent design scientists such as William Dembski[66] and Michael Behe[67] are not engaged in religion masquerading as science. Rather, they have developed criteria that can be used to identify a cause as either natural or intelligent.[68] Intelligent design should be categorized as latent Christian research because these scientists are not explicitly arguing for the God of Christianity. Rather, they are applying the canons of science to the evidence, judging the best explanation for the apparent design found in nature to be actual design. The implication of this science is clear: naturalism is false. Christianity is rendered plausible by the findings of intelligent design science. A recent example of the power of latent Christianity is the pilgrimage from atheism to theism by Antony Flew.[69] While Flew has to date only embraced an Aristotelian theism, doubtful about the possibility of special revelation and miracles (notice the influence of Hume here!), he cites arguments for intelligent design as the primary evidence causing his change in belief. Theism, and ultimately Christianity, is rendered more plausible for Flew because of the evidence for an Intelligent Designer.

But the fully integrated life of the Christian scholar is concerned with more than just the end product of research; the scholar's character is important as well. In general, Christians are called to love and seek God with all of their being. And this holistic and personal love of God by the Christian motivates our need to be both morally and intellectually virtuous. For the Christian scholar, he must not compartmentalize his academic work from his spiritual life. Christ as Lord means that he is Lord of all aspects of our lives—including

---

66. See Dembski, *Intelligent Design.*

67. See Michael Behe, *Darwin's Black Box* (New York: Free Press, 1996).

68. Dembski's criterion is called *specified complexity.* Behe's is called *irreducible complexity.*

69. Antony Flew and Gary Habermas, "My Pilgrimage from Atheism to Theism: An Exclusive Interview with Former British Atheist Professor Antony Flew," *Philosophia Christi* 6, no. 2 (2004), 197–211.

the research projects we engage in and even the very questions that we ask. It is not enough to just "be a moral Christian" or "be a faithful church attendee." Lordship unto Jesus demands that all aspects of our being, including our thought life and academic work, lead to and result in love and worship of God and others (cf. Luke 10:25–28; Matt. 22:37–39).

And there is a two-way causal connection between moral character and intellectual virtue (including one's ability to "see" the truth). A vicious moral character can undermine good thinking, and futile or lazy thinking can contribute to moral deficiencies. For example, a scholar (say, a scientist) captivated by his own pride, may lack certain intellectual virtues such as "epistemic humility" and "a love for truth" and find himself incapable of learning from experience (or younger colleagues or graduate students) or acknowledging the inadequacies of his initial beliefs should they prove wrong. And as we saw earlier, Paul agrees. Character formation requires (and begins with) a renewing of the mind: "Do not conform any longer to the pattern of this world, but be transformed by the *renewing of your mind*" (Rom. 12:2); and having "put on the new self, which is being *renewed in knowledge* in the image of its Creator" (Col. 3:10); and, "Paul, a servant of God and an apostle of Jesus Christ for the faith of God's elect and the *knowledge of the truth that leads to godliness*" (Titus 1:1).[70] While discussing the importance of the intellectual virtue of integrity for the Christian scholar, Douglas Henry states:

> [T]hough a scholar *simpliciter* aims proximately to understand, interpret, extend, or appropriate the resources of an academic discipline, a *Christian* scholar aims ultimately to express devotion to God through commitment to Christ and submission to his Spirit, and to do so qua scholar . . . a conception of Christian scholarship that focuses exclusively on content fails to recognize the wider range

---

70. Of course, this insight goes back to at least Plato and Aristotle, and was picked up and developed by many Christian thinkers in the ancient and medieval period, including Augustine and Aquinas. There has been a sort of revival in the interest of so-called virtue ethics including attention to the intellectual virtues. Two popular-level introductions to these topics of intellectual virtue are J. P. Moreland, *Love Your God with All Your Mind* (Colorado Springs: NavPress, 1997) and W. Jay Wood, *Epistemology: Becoming Intellectually Virtuous* (Downers Grove, IL: InterVarsity, 2000).

of resources needed for it to thrive. Those resources fundamentally include all the virtues.[71]

Thus, the fully integrated life is a life of intellectual and moral virtue, which ultimately is an expression and reflection of God's nature as Father, Son, and Holy Spirit as a fully integral being. Finally, in allowing the grand story of Scripture to illuminate our path, we see that Christian scholarship is never an end in itself.[72] Rather, the goal of all scholarship must be firmly placed within the framework of Scripture. While an understanding of the metanarrative of Scripture will sometimes but not always change the way we do scholarship, it will *always* change the way we view people. The *shalomic* vision of intimacy with God and harmony with each other must always be front and center in the scholarly efforts of the Christian. God is on a rescue mission, reconciling lost people back to himself (see Luke 19:10). As ambassadors of Christ (2 Cor. 5:20), we are called to participate in this mission.

The worship of God and pursuit of people are intricately related, as John Piper has so persuasively stated: "Mission is not the ultimate goal of the church. Worship is. Missions exist because worship doesn't. Worship is ultimate, not missions, because God is ultimate, not man."[73] The worship of God and pursuit of people are antithetical to the posture of the modern university. Grants, publications, institutional ranking, and individual achievement are ultimate for the university. Thus, any scholar, Christian or otherwise, who desires to succeed in mainstream academia today is tempted to make these goals ultimate as well. But for the Christian, this cannot be. God is

---

71. Douglas Henry, "Intellectual Integrity in the Christian Scholar's Life," *Christian Scholars Review* 33 (Fall 2003), 72–73.

72. While Christian scholarship is never an end in itself, it is also not merely something of instrumental value. Knowledge is an intrinsic good, and scholarship as the pursuit of knowledge is as well. However, the pursuit of knowledge ought to be viewed as a subordinate goal, good in and of itself, but subservient to the ultimate goal of the glory of God (see 1 Cor. 10:31). C. S. Lewis states this point eloquently in his address given in the fall of 1939 to students at St. Mary the Virgin Church in Oxford, England, "I mean the pursuit of knowledge and beauty, in a sense, for their own sake, but in a sense which does not exclude their being for God's sake." See C. S. Lewis, "Learning in War-Time," in *The Weight of Glory* (San Francisco: Harper Collins, 2001), 56. Thus, scholarship is something to be pursued both for its own sake and for God's sake at the same time.

73. John Piper, *Let The Nations Be Glad! The Supremacy of God in Missions* (Grand Rapids: Baker, 1993), 11.

ultimate, and God is for people. Yes, the Christian scholar should be concerned with grants, publications, individual achievement, and institutional prestige, but this concern should always be viewed within the context of service to Jesus as Lord. Perhaps the greatest test for the Christian scholar in academia today is whether or not he can trust God for his job (including tenure) while he worships God and pursues people as his ultimate priority.

The unique mode for the Christian scholar's worship of God and pursuit of people is *through his scholarly work and life*. By producing (either explicit or latent) Christian research, the Christian world and life will be restored to the status of "plausible" within the marketplace of ideas. As is well known, Christianity is no longer viewed (by many) as a plausible option today. Thus, the work of the gospel is severely hindered. As J. Gresham Machen warned in 1913:

> False ideas are the greatest obstacles to the reception of the gospel. We may preach with all the fervor of a reformer and yet succeed only in winning a straggler here and there, if we permit the whole collective thought of the nation or of the world to be controlled by ideas which, by the resistless force of logic, prevent Christianity from being regarded as anything more than a harmless delusion. Under such circumstances, what God desires us to do is destroy the obstacle at its root.[74]

The Christian scholar is on the front lines of the battle of ideas. Christian professors need to realize they are already witnesses whose lives and scholarship either help or hinder others' belief in God. If Christian professors begin to actively examine and challenge the anti-Christian assumptions within their discipline and present a winsome picture of a *whole* life, centered in God, only then can the soil be made fertile once again for the advancement of a robust view of the Christian world and life.[75]

Furthermore, Christian scholars need to work hard to resist the impulse of isolation and individualism so often engendered in academia. As ambassadors for Christ, they should look for opportunities to invite other professors (and students) into their lives. By being the hands and feet of Jesus in a world where Christ

---

74. J. Gresham Machen, "Christianity and Culture," *Princeton Theological Review* 11 (1913): 7.

75. As Marxists and feminists have shown, it only takes a committed and vocal minority to advance a particular view within academia.

is routinely ignored, ridiculed, or relegated to the private area of
life only, the Christian scholar is living Jesus' example of *going* to
the lost, *telling* the good news of the kingdom, and *showing* the
benefit of kingdom living (see Matt. 4:23; Mark 1:14–15).[76] Thus,
the Christian vision of human dignity and happiness should lead
the Christian scholar to pursue people and worship God through
his scholarly efforts as well as his life.

The Integrated Life Applied: Where We Go from Here

Each of the essays contained in this book embody and express
this integrated life. We begin with Charles Malik's original address
as delivered and subsequently published, first by Crossway (then
called Cornerstone Books) in 1980 and more recently by EMIS, the
publishing arm of the Billy Graham Center, in 2000. We believe that
the message of Dr. Malik needs to be heard again today to motivate
a new generation of Christian scholars and to encourage those who
have been faithfully serving Christ in the (often) hollow halls of
academia. Malik's message was then, and is now, a wake up call to
Christians—and especially to Christian scholars. And Malik doesn't
waste words. The battle lines are clearly drawn; the soul and mind
of men and women, even Western civilization, hangs in the balance
in an epic battle between Christ and anti-Christ, the church and the
world, a robust Christianity and anti-intellectualism and a shallow
faith. Charles Malik's words and his life leave an indelible legacy
within academia and within the church.

Charles Malik's legacy also lives on within his son, Habib, who with
the same prophetic voice and vision asks, "What then, in addition to
Charles Malik's Two Tasks . . . is required of a believing and committed
Christian in today's era of clashes?" Since its inception, Christians
have lived in a state of perpetual crisis, continually assaulted by
hostile worldviews as well as a host of spiritual challenges. Such is
the call of the Christian in a fallen world. Communism, the clash
which took up most of the twentieth century, and which Charles
Malik himself bravely fought against on the world stage, is now
largely behind us. Yet, there are new challenges today facing the
Christian believer. Habib calls to our attention six such areas of

---

76. For other examples in Scripture of the go, tell, show model to ministry,
see Luke 9:1–2; Luke 10:1, 9; and Acts 4:32–35.

conflict. First, there is the crisis of post-Christian Europe, which faces spiritual and physical demise as millions of Muslims, without any desire to assimilate into European culture, stream into the continent in search of economic prosperity. Second, there is the challenge of supporting Christians in the Middle East whose very survival is threatened on every side by oppressive regimes and extremist Islamists. This extreme and dangerous Islamism receives its own treatment by Habib, and we are reminded of the need to understand this mindset as well as to pray for the rise of a moderate Islamic voice that would speak out against this radical and violent wing within its own religion. Fourth, he discusses the importance of Russia and the Orthodox faith, reminding Western Christians of the importance of praying for and helping the Orthodox Church revive herself. Fifth, Habib discusses the culture war raging in America, reminding us once again of the need for being both media savvy and academically adept as we navigate within a culture that loves to erect simplistic caricatures of anything that smacks of Jesus Christ. Finally, Habib implores us, like his father before him, to be more ecumenical—for Catholics, Orthodox, and Protestants to find common ground and common causes and to begin to work together.

Charles Malik's two tasks message was built upon and expanded in his book, *A Christian Critique of the University*. Peter Kreeft discusses this important work, bringing his own insightful analysis and commentary to bear upon the important question asked by Malik: "What does Jesus Christ think of the university?" After discussing the importance of the university, Kreeft examines Malik's critique of the sciences and humanities, noting that many of the same criticisms apply today: pride, self-aggrandizement, skepticism, cynicism, nihilism, and hurriedness. Most helpful is Kreeft's discussion of Malik's solution to the current crisis in the university. Yes, there needs to be strategy, organization, mobilization, and moxie, but ultimately the solution involves Christian professors and scholars *being* a certain kind of person—a kind of person that Malik calls a person of being. And what is this person of being? It is the person who has Christ, who has regained his spiritual center and lives moment by moment in light of that reality.

Academics are notoriously known for being "all talk and little action." In his essay, Walter Bradley dispels that myth, sharing from a wealth of his own experience practical ways to minister to students and colleagues within academia. From student movie nights to intense group discussions with colleagues around serious Christian books, Bradley shares some "best practices" that he has learned over his nearly forty years as a university professor. Even such mundane things as building a bridge are turned, in the hands of Christians like Bradley, into opportunities to be the hands and feet of Jesus to a lost and needy world. Endearingly, Bradley brings to our attention something I suspect is true for many great men and women of faith in the university—behind the university professor is a spouse praying, sharing, and co-laboring in the work of the gospel to these same students, colleagues, and significant others, and in the process providing a more complete picture of the Christian world and life to a secular mindset desperately (even if unknowingly) in need of such a vision. May we all, along with Dr. Bradley, be able to look forward, at the end of our career, and one day, our life, to that final "post tenure review" in heaven with humble assurance.

But while all university professors have much in common, there are still some great divides—most notably between the sciences and humanities. In chapter 6, Princeton physicist Robert Kaita expertly discusses some of the unique challenges and opportunities of being a Christian scientist (not a follower of Mary Baker Eddy!) in the academy today. Kaita begins by discussing Paul's speech on Mars Hill in Athens as an example of a heuristic approach to evangelism in academia. Sensitivity to the biases, beliefs, and values of our audience are critical in deciding how we ought to communicate the timeless truths of the gospel. This need for sensitivity is evident in the raging and often emotional battle over intelligent design and evolution. Kaita brings to our attention the fact that many times even scientists are talking past each other—for words such as "theory" and "science" mean very different things to, for example, biologist and physicist. And these semantic differences have very practical implications in various issues regarding faith, science, and the relationship between the two. But, faith and science, the book of Scripture and the book of nature, come, as Kaita reminds us, from the same God, and both reveal him in a unique way. And with both of these "books," as with the two tasks, there is a common need to communicate in a language and life that can be heard by its audience. Kaita's chapter helps us to see how this can be done.

The humanities are often beguiled by a different set of issues, most notably a postmodern mindset that seeks to "deconstruct" the text and rip it from its historical context and its intended authorial meaning. The result is that students (and professors) in the humanities, as John North points out in chapter 7, have become victims of many competing voices. Yet within the "canonical" text of the humanities, if we allow it to speak for itself, we find the voice of God speaking to the angst and longings of the human heart. King Lear asks, "Who is it who can tell me who I am?" This question, which as North points out is really everyone's question, is answered within each discipline of the humanities (i.e., the voice of God is present, if we allow it to be heard). Most notable in North's essay, however, is his passion to faithfully live out the two tasks within the context of academia; his many personal stories of interaction with students and colleagues serves both as a challenge and example of what a fully integrated life can look like within the university.

In chapter 8, William Lane Craig offers some final thoughts on the two great tasks of the Christian scholar. After reviewing the nature of the battle and need for Christian scholars to live fully integrated lives, Craig gets very practical. First, Christian scholars should engage intellectually, not only with their chosen discipline, but with the Christian faith as well. Gone are the days of the polymath. Instead, university professors have often become so specialized that all other intellectual domains, including one's faith, become increasingly neglected. The result for the Christian professor is often minimal knowledge of Scripture and theology. Craig offers sound advice to help Christian professors begin to attend to the intellectual component of the Christian faith. Second, Craig emphasizes again the importance of integrating one's Christian faith with one's discipline. And finally, Craig encourages us to be mindful of our personal, spiritual formation unto Christ.

I offer one final thought, actually a reminder of a God-placed longing I think we all tend to forget as the burdens and responsibilities and wounds of life multiply upon us over time. And this longing is best expressed through the mouth of my seven-year-old son, Austin. One night, as I was tucking Austin into bed, he asked, "Dad, would you rather die as a hero by saving someone else or die of old age?" I thought for a minute before answering, and then said, "I would rather die of old age than to die a hero's death saving someone, but if called upon to do so, I hope I would have the courage to be the hero God wants me to be." And then I said, "But Austin, I think you are actually asking two questions, for in your question you are also asking, how can one *live* a heroic life? And the answer to *that* question is to allow your life to be a sacrifice daily to God, to live a life where Jesus is your King and Master." I believe that the deep undercurrent in my son's question expresses the same question and longing we all have: is Jesus really the answer in death *and* life? In these pages, you will read of battle-tested wisdom and insight from men who are living heroic lives. You will also hear of many other men and women who are living heroic lives in which they daily die to self on the front line in the battle for the souls of others, embracing Malik's vision of Christian wholeness and leadership in the university. May we all have the courage and grace to follow their example as we look to Christ.

Discussion Questions

1. How do the two tasks relate to a fully integrated life for the Christian scholar?

2. What are some other highlights of Christian scholars or scholarship that you are aware of since Malik's 1980 message? Lowlights? In your own institution?

3. Is there a para-church ministry on your campus or in your region that you can partner with? Is there a Christian study center on your campus? If not, what could that look like at your university?

4. Gould describes graduate school as a "bootcamp" where the university conforms you into its own image. How was your graduate experience? How can you help encourage Christian graduate students today?

5. Why is an understanding of God's larger story important to the task of integration? Does any specific aspect of the metanarrative play a more crucial role in your discipline?

6. Why does our view of Jesus as smart, or intellectually virtuous, matter?

7. Do you agree that Christians should be principled pluralists within secular academia? Why or why not?

8. Is your research mostly explicitly Christian or latently Christian (in either the implicit sense or the purely vocational sense)?

9. In what ways is your discipline in need of transformation?

10. Do you see the university as a mission field? Review how God called you into the academy.

2

THE TWO TASKS

CHARLES MALIK

speak to you as a Christian. Jesus Christ is my Lord and God and Savior and Song day and night. I can live without food, without drink, without sleep, without air, but I cannot live without Jesus. Without him I would have perished long ago. Without him and his church reconciling man to God, the world would have perished long ago. I live in and on the Bible for long hours every day. The Bible is the source of every good thought and impulse I have. In the Bible God himself, the Creator of everything from nothing, speaks to me and to the world directly, about himself, about ourselves, and about his will for the course of events and for the consummation of history. And believe me, not a day passes without my crying from the bottom of my heart, "Come, Lord Jesus!" I know he is coming with glory to judge the living and the dead, but in my impatience I sometimes cannot wait, and I find myself in my infirmity crying with David, "How long, Lord?" And I know his kingdom shall have no end.

I apologize for this personal witness and I know you will take it with a charitable heart.

The Spiritual Side of the Problem

Nothing is as important in the world today as for the Christians of America to grasp their historic opportunities and prove themselves equal to them. I say "the Christians," but I must add also "the Jews," because what is fatefully at stake today is the highest spiritual values of the Judaeo-Christian tradition. If the highest Christian values are overturned, so will the highest Jewish values.

Perhaps never since the twelve disciples and Saint Paul has any group of Christians been burdened by Providence itself with the responsibilities now devolving upon the Christians of America.

By "Christians" I mean at once the Protestants, the Catholics, and the Orthodox. The intensity of conviction, suffering, and witness being evidenced today in the Orthodox world, especially in Russia, is something for which the living Lord must be profoundly thanked. The Catholics, under the eminent leadership of that remarkable man, John Paul II, are manifesting an immense vitality all over the world. But materially, politically, and morally, the Protestants of America command absolutely unprecedented resources, and spiritually they are in a state of creative ferment. In one brief sentence Billy Graham expressed this in his message on the occasion of the groundbreaking ceremony for this center on September 28, 1977, when he said: "We have greater opportunities, greater challenges, greater needs than at any time in history."

What together, not separately but together, and in sincere cooperation with other Christians, the Protestants of America can do today for the promotion of the highest interests of man and the spirit, in the media, in the schools and universities, in the churches themselves, in the seminaries, in individual personal character, in popular literature, in the conduct of business, in the councils of the state, in international relations, and in the general quality of life of a whole epoch, is more, by far, than any other group of Christians can effect. And so the burden of their infinite accountability before God and history can only be carried at once with the deepest joy and the most authentic humility.

Protestantism emphasizes four fundamental truths: the supreme importance of the Bible, both Old and New Testaments, as the Word of God; Jesus Christ of Nazareth as the living Lord of lords and King of kings, with whom we must, and indeed we can, have a direct personal relationship; justification by faith and not by works, which is best expressed by Romans 4:5 (KJV), "But to him that worketh not, but believeth on him that justifieth the ungodly, his faith is counted for righteousness"; and individual, personal, responsible freedom as the very essence of the dignity of man.

The year 1983 marks the five hundredth anniversary of the birth of Martin Luther. During these five centuries the four basic affirmations of the Reformation have permeated the entire Christian world. Who among the faithful in all branches of Christianity today is not reading the Bible, or is prevented or discouraged from reading it? Who does not live, in some sense, in the presence of Jesus, the living Lord? Who, knowing his own inveterate rottenness, and knowing it invariably precisely when he is at his best, expects to be saved by his sanctity only or by the merits of his works? And who is not placing freedom of thought, conscience, choice, and belief at the heart of all clamor for human rights? The Reformation has made its point.

Who therefore can predict today what may not be celebrated precisely on the occasion of the five hundredth anniversary of the birth of Martin Luther three years from now, in terms of closer understanding, and therefore mutual appreciation and forgiveness, between Protestantism on the one hand and Catholicism and Orthodoxy on the other? "O the depth of the riches both of the wisdom and knowledge of God! how unsearchable are his judgments, and his ways past finding out! For who hath known the mind of the Lord? or who hath been his counselor?" (Rom. 11:33–34, KJV).

For the Protestants, therefore, to be able to fulfill their appointed destiny, now that their four distinctive emphases are universally accepted and absorbed, it would seem three requirements are necessary: greater unity among themselves (some of them are hardly on speaking terms with others); greater understanding and mutual toleration between the evangelicals among them (although all Christians, by definition, are evangelical) and the more established churches; and rediscovering and appropriating the infinite riches of the great traditions: Orthodox, Catholic, and Protestant. On the first two points, Billy Graham, with his spirit and his name, and the center named after him here, may be called to play a leading role.

On the third point, when Catholics sing in their churches "A Mighty Fortress Is Our God" as lustily as it is sung by the lustiest Lutherans, you feel we are already in a new age. Consequently I ask: who could possibly be harmed or impoverished, from the point of view of knowing and loving and worshiping Jesus Christ, if he

knew something authentic about St. Ignatius of Antioch, or St. John
Chrysostom, or St. Basil the Great, or St. Ephrem, or St. Augustine,
or St. Thomas Aquinas, or St. Teresa of Avila? I assure you these
are among the greatest Christians of all time, and Protestants will
not be polluted if they steep themselves in them.

And yet there are people who are offended by the mere mention
of the word "Saint," especially when written with a capital "S"!
Having regard to the infinitely serious issues at stake, I trust this
particular human offense will be transcended.

There are also some who affect to think that nothing really worth
knowing happened in the Christian world between Saint Paul and
Billy Graham. I know Billy Graham is a landmark, but not a landmark
to the extent that everything between him and Saint Paul has been
a total blank. Jesus Christ, who is the light of the world, will not be
revealed as such, and his wonderful light will not shine in the awful
darkness of our world, until the American evangelicals, on whom so
much depends today, integrate into themselves, and get themselves
integrated into, the unity and continuity of the cumulative Christian
tradition. He has shone on many a soul and many a culture in the
past, and not only on the evangelicals of today.

What could not be achieved for the glory of God and the name
of Jesus Christ, and indeed for peace and understanding among
all men, if the principle of freedom, which is of course sacred and
primordial, did not obliterate or unduly interfere with the principle of
solidarity and cooperation and mutual trust and forbearance, which
is also primordial, and if the dimension of history is confidently
opened wide and the cumulative tradition understood and loved
and claimed? For us men in this vale of tears there is more than
just God and the Bible and you as an individual person at this very
moment: there are also others, both in time and space; and it is
communion with others across the ages that is more sorely needed
today than even communion with others in our time.

The Intellectual Side of the Problem

This is the spiritual side of the problem; there is also the intellectual
side.

In the nature of the case, evangelization is always the most
important task to be undertaken by mortal man. For proud and
rebellious and self-sufficient man—and pride and rebellion and self-

sufficiency are the same thing—to be brought to his knees and to his tears before the actual majesty and grace and power of Jesus Christ is the greatest event that can happen to any man. Indeed, just as every man is ordained to die, so every man is ordained to this event happening in his own life. And those who are engaged in mediating this event, the evangelists, are the supreme heralds of God.

But just as we are not alone with God and the Bible but also with others, so we are not only endowed with a soul and a will to be saved but also with a reason to be sharpened and satisfied. This reason wonders about everything, including God, and we are to seek and love and worship the Lord our God with all our strength and all our mind. And because we are with others we are arguing and reasoning with one another all the time. Indeed every sentence and every discourse is a product of reason. And so it is neither a shame nor a sin to discipline and cultivate our reason to the utmost; it is a necessity, it is a duty, it is an honor to do so.

Therefore, if evangelization is the most important task, the task that comes immediately after it—not in the tenth place, nor even the third place, but in the second place—is not politics, nor economics, nor the quest for comfort and security and ease, but to find out exactly what is happening to the mind and the spirit in the schools and universities. And once a Christian discovers that there is a total divorce between mind and spirit in the schools and universities, between the perfection of thought and the perfection of soul and character, between intellectual sophistication and the spiritual worth of the individual human person, between reason and faith, between the pride of knowledge and the contrition of heart consequent upon being a mere creature, and once he realizes that Jesus Christ will find himself less at home on the campuses of the great universities in Europe and America than almost anywhere else, he will be profoundly disturbed, and he will inquire what can be done to recapture the great universities for Jesus Christ, the universities which would not have come into being in the first place without him.

What can the poor church, even at its best, do; what can evangelization, even at its most inspired, do; what can the poor family, even at its purest and noblest, do, if the children spend between fifteen and twenty years of their life, and indeed the most formative period of their life, in school and college in an atmosphere of formal denial of any relevance of God and spirit and soul and faith to the formation of their mind? The enormity of what is happening is beyond words.

The church and the family, each already encumbered with its own strains and ordeals, are fighting a losing battle, so far as the bearing of the university upon the spiritual health and wholeness of youth is concerned. All the preaching in the world, and all the loving care of even the best parents between whom there are no problems whatever, will amount to little, if not to nothing, so long as what the children are exposed to day in and day out for fifteen to twenty years in the school and university virtually cancels out, morally and spiritually, what they hear and see and learn at home and in the church. Therefore the problem of the school and university is the most critical problem afflicting Western civilization. And here we meet laughing and relaxing and enjoying ourselves and celebrating as though nothing of this order of gravity were happening!

I assure you, so far as the university is concerned, I have no patience with piety alone—I want the most rigorous intellectual training, I want the perfection of the mind; equally, I have no patience with reason—I want the salvation of the soul, I want the fear of the Lord, I want at least neutrality with respect to the knowledge of Jesus Christ.

What I crave to see is an institution that will produce as many Nobel Prize winners as saints, an institution in which, while producing in every field the finest works of thought and learning in the world, Jesus Christ will at the same time find himself perfectly at home in it—in every dormitory and lecture hall and library and laboratory. This is impossible today. Why it is impossible, is the most important question that can be asked.

The sciences are flourishing as never before, and may they keep on flourishing and exploding and discovering!

And lest I be misunderstood, let me state at once that I consider Freiburg, the Sorbonne, Harvard, Princeton, and Chicago among the greatest—and some of them the greatest—universities in the world, and, provided my children qualify, I would certainly send them to them. The diversity and quality of the intellectual fare available to the student in these universities is absolutely unprecedented in history. Western civilization can be proud of many things; of nothing it can be more proud than of its great universities.

But I am worried about the humanities—about philosophy, psychology, art, history, literature, sociology, the interpretation of man as to his nature and his destiny. It is in these realms that the spirit, the fundamental attitude, the whole outlook on life, even for the scientist himself, are formed and set. Nor am I unaware and unappreciative of the great advances achieved in the methods, techniques, and tools of education, and in the remarkable enlargement of the scope of the curriculum. But in terms of content and substance, what is the dominant philosophy in the humanities today?

We find on the whole and for the most part: materialism and hedonism; naturalism and rationalism; relativism and Freudianism; a great deal of cynicism and nihilism; indifferentism and atheism; linguistic analysis and radical obfuscation; immanentism and the absence of any sense of mystery, any sense of wonder, any sense of tragedy; humanism and self-sufficiency; the worship of the future, not of something above and outside and judging past, present, and future; the relative decay of the classics; the uncritical worship of everything new and modern and different; a prevailing false conception of progress; an uncritical and almost childish optimism; an uncritical and morbid pessimism; the will to power and domination. All of which are essentially so many modes of self-worship. Any wonder there is so much disorder in the world!

If what I say is true, then as Christians you should not be able to sleep, not only tonight but for a whole week. But I know you are going to sleep very soundly tonight, probably because you do not believe me, probably because you do not care!

At the heart of all the problems facing Western civilization—the general nervousness and restlessness, the dearth of grace and beauty and quiet and peace of soul, the manifold blemishes and perversion of personal character, problems of the family and of social relations in general, problems of economics and politics, problems of the media, problems affecting the school itself and the church itself, problems in the international order—at the heart of the crisis in Western civilization lies the state of the mind and the spirit in the universities.

It is totally vain, it is indeed childish, to tackle these problems as though all were well, in morals and in the fundamental orientation of the will and mind, in the great halls of learning. Where do the leaders in these realms come from? They all come from universities. What they are fed, intellectually, morally, spiritually, personally, in the fifteen or twenty years they spend in the school and university, is the decisive question. It is there that the foundations of character and mind and outlook and conviction and attitude and spirit are laid, and, to paraphrase a biblical saying, if the wrong foundations are laid, or if the right foundations are vitiated or undermined, "what can the righteous do?" (Ps. 11:3, KJV).

Of course at this point the charge of self-righteousness will be leveled. But the question is so momentous that it must be vigorously raised even at the risk of this charge and of a dozen other charges and misunderstandings.

If there are three billion dollars to be thrown away—and, if not every day or every week, at least every month three billion dollars are being thrown away—let them go to founding and supporting some kind of institute whose sole aim is to find out the truth of what is happening in the humanities in the great universities of Europe and America.

The finest minds must be enlisted—philosophers, scientists, poets, theologians, preachers, cardinals, bishops, university presidents, presidents of republics, presidents of corporations—twenty at most and only five to begin with. They may include two or three non-Christians, but all the rest must be dedicated Christians. Their mandate is twofold: to produce by the end of this decade the most objective, exhaustive, and thorough study of what is really happening in the great universities of Europe and America in the field of the humanities, and to suggest practical ways and means for permeating that field with the right spirit, the right attitude, in a word, with right reason.

This is a Christian undertaking. Secularist-rationalist-humanist experimentation with liberal education is going on all the time, and only last year a great university put forward its own project. Christ being the light of the world, his light must be brought to bear on the problem of the formation of the mind. The investigation will have to be accomplished with the utmost discretion and humility, and it can only be carried out by men of prayer and faith. Once the light of Christ is shed on this study, incalculable will be the light the study itself will shed on all problems facing the Western world.

The thing is not mechanical nor is it a question of reforming the university; the university only reflects the mind of contemporary culture; we are dealing here with a thoroughgoing critique, from the point of view of Jesus Christ, of Western civilization as to its highest contemporary values. This is what lends this task its grandeur and its supreme responsibility.

I regret this is all abstract thinking, and nothing is more hateful to me that this kind of thinking. But I wanted only to pose the problem. Believe me, my friends, the mind today is in profound trouble, perhaps more so than ever before. How to order the mind on sound Christian principles at the very heart of where it is formed and informed, namely, in the universities, is one of the two greatest themes that can be considered. While we are living "between the times," I mean, between the first and the second coming of Jesus Christ, and while human society continues to be under the sway of terrible sin and corruption, this theme must engage us with the utmost urgency.

The problem is not only to win souls but to save minds. If you win the whole world and lose the mind of the world, you will soon discover you have not won the world. Indeed it may turn out that you have actually lost the world.

In order to create and excel intellectually, must you sacrifice or neglect Jesus? In order to give all your life to Jesus, must you sacrifice or neglect learning and research? Is your self-giving to scholarship and learning essentially incompatible with your self-giving to Jesus Christ? These are the ultimate questions, and I beg you to beware of thinking that they admit of glib answers. I warn you: the right answer could be most disturbing.

Could the Billy Graham Center at Wheaton College sponsor this task? It remains to be seen whether it could. But if Christians do not care for the intellectual health of their own children and for the fate of their own civilization, a health and a fate so inextricably bound up with the state of the mind and spirit in the universities, who is going to care? The task is gigantic, and for it to be accomplished as I believe Christ himself would want it to be accomplished, people must be set on fire for it. It is not enough to be set on fire for evangelization alone.

This is a solemn occasion. I must be frank with you: the great danger besetting American Evangelical Christianity is the danger of anti-intellectualism. The mind as to its greatest and deepest reaches is not cared for enough. This cannot take place apart from profound immersion for a period of years in the history of thought and the spirit.

People are in a hurry to get out of the university and start earning money or serving the church or preaching the gospel. They have no idea of the infinite value of spending years of leisure in conversing with the greatest minds and souls of the past, and thereby ripening and sharpening and enlarging their powers of thinking. The result is that the arena of creative thinking is abdicated and vacated to the enemy. Who among the evangelicals can stand up to the great secular or naturalistic or atheistic scholars on their own terms of scholarship and research? Who among the evangelical scholars is quoted as a normative source by the greatest secular authorities on history or philosophy or psychology or sociology or politics? Does your mode of thinking have the slightest chance of becoming the dominant mode of thinking in the great universities of Europe and America which stamp your entire civilization with their own spirit and ideas?

It will take a different spirit altogether to overcome this great danger of anti-intellectualism. As an example only, I say this different spirit, so far as the domain of philosophy alone is concerned, which is the most important domain so far as thought and intellect are concerned, must see the tremendous value of spending a whole year doing nothing except poring intensely over the *Republic* or the *Sophist* of Plato, or two years over the *Metaphysics* or the *Ethics* of Aristotle, or three years over the *City of God* of Augustine. Even if you start now on a crash program in this and other domains, it will be a century at least before you catch up with the Harvards and Tübingens and the Sorbonnes, and think of where these universities will be then. For the sake of greater effectiveness in witnessing to Jesus Christ himself, as well as for their own sakes, the evangelicals cannot afford to keep on living on the periphery of responsible intellectual existence.

In the short time allotted to me I am only here to intimate and point out: I am not to expound. But the real meat and marrow come only in the expounding.

Responsible Christians face two tasks—that of saving the soul and that of saving the mind. I am using soul and mind here without definition, but I can define them in precise, philosophical-theological terms. The mind is desperately disordered today. I am pleading that a tiny fraction of Christian care be extended to the mind too. If it is the will of the Holy Ghost that we attend to the soul, certainly it is not his will that we neglect the mind. No civilization can endure with its mind being as confused and disordered as ours is today. All our ills stem proximately from the false philosophies that have been let loose in the world and that are now being taught in the universities, and ultimately of course, as your President Armerding observes in his book *Leadership* in another context, from the devil,

whether or not the human agents knew it. Save the university and
you save Western civilization and therewith the world.

What could be more wonderful than for a center named after the
greatest evangelist of our age to aim at achieving, under God and
according to God's own pace, the twofold miracle of evangelizing
the great universities and intellectualizing the great Evangelical
movement? These two things are absolutely impossible, and because
they are at the same time absolutely needed, God can make them
absolutely possible.

Every self-defeating attitude stems originally from the devil,
because he is the adversary, the arch-nihilist *par excellence*. It cannot
be willed by the Holy Ghost. Anti-intellectualism is an absolutely
self-defeating attitude. Wake up, my friends, wake up: the great
universities control the mind of the world. Therefore how can
evangelism consider its task accomplished if it leaves the university
unevangelized? And how can evangelism evangelize the university
if it cannot speak to the university? And how can it speak to the
university if it is not itself already intellectualized?

Therefore evangelism must first intellectualize itself to be able
to speak to the university and therefore to be able to evangelize the
university and therefore to save the world. This is the great task,
the historic task, the most needed task, the task required loud and
clear by the Holy Ghost himself, to which the Billy Graham Center
must humbly address itself.

And if this should happen, then think of the infinite joy that would
overflow our hearts. Future generations will bless your name and sing
your praises for centuries to come. Who, then, would not join with
David in singing, "Bless the Lord, O my soul: and all that is within
me, bless his holy name. Bless the Lord, O my soul, and forget not all
his benefits. . . . I will sing unto the Lord as long as I live: I will sing
praise to my God while I have my being" (Ps. 103:1–2; 104:33, kjv).

Discussion Questions

1. Malik emphasized the importance of Christians working
   together.

   • How can Christian professors come together at your institu-
     tion for the cause of Christ?

   • How can Christian professors come together within your
     discipline for the cause of Christ?

2. Have Protestants invested their spiritual and financial resources wisely over the past twenty-five years?

   • What are some areas of opportunity today for American Protestants?

   • How can Christians from the three great traditions—Protestant, Catholic, and Orthodox—work together to further God's kingdom within academia today?

3. How does the university foster "pride and self-sufficiency"?

4. Malik said the most critical problem afflicting Western civilization is the schools and universities. Do you agree with this comment today? Why or why not?

5. What do you think of Malik's suggestion to form a distinctly Christian institute "whose sole aim is to find out the truth of what is happening in the humanities," to conduct "a thorough-going critique, from the point of view of Jesus Christ" within academia? How could this help further the cause of Christ? Is there anything like this today? Is there anything like this today asking the same kind of question of the sciences?

6. Malik's ultimate question: "In order to create and excel intellectually, must you sacrifice or neglect Jesus?" Discuss.

7. Malik's question: "Who among the evangelical scholars is quoted as a normative source by the greatest secular authorities on history or philosophy or psychology or sociology or politics?" How would you answer this question for these disciplines? For your own? How is the presence of top Christian academics having a leavening effect with the academy?

8. Malik is issuing a wake-up call for Christians. How, in concrete terms, can you apply his message?

Editors Note: Copies of the entire address are available in booklet form from EMIS (Evangelism and Missions Information Service), Billy Graham Center, 500 College Avenue, Wheaton, IL 60187, EMIS@wheaton.edu, and EMISDirect. com.

3

THE TWO TASKS REVISITED: BEING A CHRISTIAN IN THE ERA OF CIVILIZATION CLASHES

HABIB C. MALIK

Being a Christian in the era of civilization clashes? As if there has ever been a period in history free of such clashes! Confrontations with evil and the ensuing spiritual crises that such confrontations spawn have been with Christians ever since the earliest times. These conflicts have usually involved clashes between the opposing values of Christians on the one hand, and pagans or other belief systems on the other. The first three hundred years saw the followers of the new creed out of Palestine persecuted by the pagan Romans and a variety of gnostic cults and other heresies. In AD 410, after Alaric and his Visigoths sacked Rome, fleeing pagans streaming into North Africa carried horror stories of what had happened and blamed Christianity for the disaster, which in turn prompted the Bishop of Hippo, St. Augustine, to write a massive defense of Christianity—his famous *City of God*—that also turned out to be an elaborate theology of history complete with an exhaustive ecclesiology and a treatment of the problem of evil.

In the first half of the seventh century a new challenge emerged out of Arabia in the form of the early Islamic conquests that quickly reached southern France after overrunning North Africa and the Iberian Peninsula. Seen from an early Christian perspective, Islam was, in a basic sense, the return of the Arian heresy (the revenge of Arius, so to speak). Arianism, the denial of the divinity of Christ, had been condemned by the church at the Council of Nicea in AD 325. The response of Christian Europe to these Islamic conquests came some centuries later in the form of the Crusades—waves of counterattacks into the Levant with a view to reclaim control over Christianity's holy places. The Mongol invasions and then the Ottoman conquests that followed brought new civilizational challenges to European Christendom. And then, after a period of introspection in which Christians wrestled with their own shortcomings and produced both the Reformation and Counterreformation, the civilizational clash was internalized, and renewed challenges came from the deism of the eighteenth century, varieties of atheism, and lastly the secular humanism of the contemporary West.

Christian believers, therefore, have been embattled in every age, because in every age there has been a civilization clash of sorts involving one assault or other on Christian beliefs and values. A historian once half-seriously tallied the number of years throughout recorded history when there were no documented instances of conflicts or wars—they came out to some forty years of peace altogether. The world's current preoccupation with the World Cup does not mean a cessation of wars![1] But even during such rare periods of no direct hostilities, culture wars and battles of ideas and spiritual challenges rage on. Whether we choose to call it a clash of civilizations, or of cultures, or of values; or whether it is a clash between civilized existence as such on the one hand and varieties of barbarism on the other; or whether still it is a clash *within* a particular civilization between, say, fanaticism and moderation, Christians have lived in a perpetual state of crisis resulting from recurring assaults by hostile worldviews and sometimes directly by the devil himself. Hence there is the abiding depth and relevance for individual Christians and Christian communities alike of, for instance, Karl Barth's "Crisis Theology," with its emphasis on the

---

1. On July 12, 2006, two weeks after Habib Malik delivered the speech on which this chapter is based, war again broke out in Malik's native homeland of Lebanon.

continuous struggle with sin and with our fallen state. This is the ultimate meaning of the cross for us Christians.

Today, Christians have just emerged successfully from a clash that took up most of the twentieth century: the challenge of communism. But it was a debilitating clash, and after having also disposed of Nazism at tremendous costs, we are facing a new (but at the same time an old and familiar) threat: the challenge of *Islamism*, or *radical jihadist Islam*. These are the two broad titles of this latest phase of the perennial struggle—along with, of course, the ongoing culture war right here in our very midst that threatens to undermine everything we as Christians hold dear to our hearts. The culture war includes the combined assaults of materialism and hedonism, the myth of human self-sufficiency, relativism and subjectivism, scientism and technologism, atheism, indifferentism, and so on. Communism and Islamism, however, are two very different threats. While communism was an atheistic materialist ideology attempting in vain to overthrow religion and obliterate spirituality, Islamism is an extremist interpretation of a 1,400-year old religion and as such represents a spiritual challenge of a far more potent nature. Moreover, Islamism entails a belief system that does not hesitate to embrace death. Specifically, the Islamist seeks to go to paradise by sending you to hell! As Michael Ignatieff recently put it, when someone is fighting you eschatologically like the suicide bomber, what do you do? You have to protect yourself, and that may mean you have to kill him first—no room here for half-measures or for romantic pacifism.[2]

What then, in addition to Charles Malik's two tasks (attention to the soul and the mind), is required of a believing and committed Christian in today's era of clashes? In fact, there are multiple civilizational challenges and frontiers of confrontation, a number of them directly related to Islamism, and some by way of internal housekeeping. I will concentrate on six areas that require the special attention of the Christian believer in today's world and in the foreseeable future.

The Crisis of Europe

Europe is experiencing profound malaise as a civilization. It has largely become post-Christian, and what is worse is that it embraces

---

2. See Michael Ignatieff, "Lesser Evils," *New York Times Magazine*, May 2, 2004.

this self-inflicted state for the most part willingly. Is Europe then slowly perishing? Even the thought of such a question makes one shudder. Not long ago a question like this was inconceivable. If one's categories of evaluation are EU expansion and overall EU economic performance, then such a question at this juncture would sound absurd. But these are surely not my categories. For a long time the West was defined mainly by Europe, and it was at the zenith of its power and creativity and assertiveness. But most importantly, it was at the height of self-confidence: the selfless missionaries, the material and scientific progress, the aesthetic achievements, the moral message of the West, the living spiritual deposit of centuries of piety and toil—all stood for something good and universal. Napoleon invaded Egypt in 1798, which represented a wake-up call for Muslims. The Ottoman Empire was progressively failing while Europe was leaping ahead. Then came the two world wars and decolonization, and there crept in self-doubt resulting in a gradual loss of nerve— most alarmingly, a loss of faith. Early on in his pontificate, Pope John Paul II mentioned an urgent task that faced the church and Christians generally: the need to re-evangelize Europe. The "re" is crucial because one is not dealing here with a tabula rasa or some terra incognita, but with Europe where Christianity has imprinted itself on people's lives for at least a millennium and a half. The late pope's call has been taken up by leading American Catholic thinkers like George Weigel in *The Cube and the Cathedral: Europe, America, and Politics without God*, Father Richard John Neuhaus of *First Things*, Mary Ann Glendon of Harvard Law School, and others. But the actual task of re-evangelization of Europe remains in the embryonic stages. Hardly anything could be more urgent. Praying for Europe is vital as is writing about its spiritual crisis, but actually going into the field to re-evangelize is indispensable.

What are the alarming signs that characterize post-Christian Europe, and how does this situation compare with matters across the Atlantic in the United States? What is said here must be taken as delineating disturbing broad trends, but there are of course pleasant exceptions everywhere:

- Europeans are ashamed of their Christian heritage; in fact, they hate it. The EU refused to include any reference to "Judeo-Christian heritage" in the new European constitu- tion—a cumbersome and unwieldy document. This is to deny a glaring historical fact that the last 1,500 years, if not more, in Europe were profoundly shaped by the enormous impact of that tradition and heritage. Burning incense blindly at the twin altars of multiculturalism and political correctness, plus a pervasive and increasingly virulent secularism, stand conspicuously behind the feelings of shame with respect to this Christian identity.

- Europeans are not having enough babies. Negative growth has been registered in Italy and France, and in other parts demographic increase is at an all-time low. Compare that to the far healthier statistics in the United States, now having passed the three hundred million population mark. The difference is evident throughout Europe, particularly at children's playgrounds where there usually are not the throngs of kids crowding the slides and swings that one sees across America. One disturbing though somewhat sensationalized study by a Russia watcher who is a demographic specialist concluded that if present trends of decline continue, in less than forty years the majority in Russia will be Muslims.[3] Europe is fast becoming a continent of senior citizens with all the attendant socio-economic consequences that entails.

- There is loss of Christian faith across the board in Europe. Many in Europe have decided to "go it alone"—without God and without their Christian heritage. Churches in many urban areas throughout the continent are more like museums than living places of worship, or they display an aging and dwindling attendance as things were under communism. In America, on the other hand, a medium-sized family arriving late for Sunday worship would likely have a

---

3. He is Paul Goble, vice dean of social sciences and humanities at Concordia-Audentes University in Tallinn, Estonia, and formerly a U.S. government official for twenty-five years. See Meredith Buel, "Analyst Predicts Muslim Majority in Russia within Thirty Years," *Voice of America*, February 28, 2006, http://www.voanews.com/English/2006-02-28_voa77.cfm (accessed October 15, 2006). See also "Russia Challenged by Coming Muslim Majority, Expert Says," *Radio Free Europe/Radio Liberty*, March 6, 2006, http://www.referl.org/releases/2006/03/389-060306.asp (accessed October 15, 2006). Viktor Perevedentsev, who has been studying Russian population trends since the 1960s, disagrees with Goble and regards his predictions as highly inflated. See Steven Eke, "Russia Faces Demographic Disaster," *BBC News*, Moscow, June 7, 2006, http://www.bbc.co.uk/news (accessed October 15, 2006).

hard time finding empty places in the crowded pews. Church
attendance is still robust in the United States compared to
that in large parts of Europe.

• Whenever Europe needs cheap labor it looks to the neigh-
boring Islamic regions such as North Africa, Turkey, and
other parts of the Middle East. The result has been an influx
of Muslims into Europe in the millions, and many of these
are coming in not in order to assimilate, but as settlers. One
scholar has called it a "demographic jihad."[4] Worse still, the
Europeans (especially the French) are in denial and turn a
blind eye to this phenomenon, explaining it in purely socio-
economic terms with hardly any reference to the underly-
ing cultural and religious components. Muslims streaming
into France are hardly arriving in order to embrace French
laicisme! Couple this phenomenon with the potential entry
of Turkey into the EU and one has the makings of the end of
European civilization as we have known it. Assisting Turkey's
entry into the EU is therefore tantamount to murder, or suicide if you are a European. Already America's record in the
Balkans during the 1990s in helping to assert the Islamic identity of certain parts there has been shameful. Contrast all this
with the United States' domestic need for cheap labor, which
is obtained mostly from south of the border, and one sees
the steady influx of Catholic Hispanics who share the same
overall worldview with the vast majority of Americans.

• Features of what is best termed the "culture of death" are
taking hold of parts of Europe (and to a lesser extent, the
United States): abortion, euthanasia, assisted suicides,
homosexuality leading to legalized same-sex unions, and
genetic manipulation. The difference between both sides of
the Atlantic on this issue is that in the Unites States there are
at least moves afoot in society to openly resist this creeping
culture of death, whereas in Europe such resistance is weak
if not non-existent.

Europe matters for Christians and Christianity. The spiritual,
and eventually physical, demise of Europe before this multi-

---

4. See Robert Spencer, *Islam Unveiled: Disturbing Questions about the World's
Fastest-Growing Faith* (San Francisco: Encounter Books, 2002), 170–73.

pronged onslaught would constitute a calamity of historic—indeed apocalyptic—proportions. We cannot allow this to happen. The only antidote is an aggressive, sustained, and earnest re-evangelization of the afflicted continent—a rearguard action to shore up our fraying civilizational flanks. This has now become a more urgent task than evangelizing any other part of the world. The big question remains: will re-evangelization bear quick enough fruits to save Europe?

The Embattled Christians of the Middle East

The cradle of Christianity is steadily emptying out. Christians native to the region where it all began are leaving in growing numbers. The reasons are simple: persecution and being caught between repressive regimes on one side and rising Islamist radicalism and fanaticism on the other; lack of security and no clear future prospects; dwindling economic opportunities; the allure of the West where assimilation seems relatively easy; and low birth rates—certainly lower than those of Muslims who can marry up to four wives and who can divorce much more easily than Christians. Apart from the purely humanitarian side of the issue where the depletion of any group due to the reasons cited is something worthy of the attention of Christians, and apart even from the fact that in this case the disappearing groups are coreligionists, there is a practical policy-related matter that must be considered: secure, free, and prosperous indigenous Christian communities living in their ancestral homes throughout the Middle East will help promote Islamic moderation and foster respect for ethno-religious pluralism in the face of both the oppressive regimes and the extremist Islamists.

There are two distinct historical narratives for Middle Eastern Christians: the vast majority (over 90 percent of them) fell at one point or other during the last 1,400 years under direct Islamic subjugation and became *dhimmis*, or second-class citizens. These include the Copts of Egypt and the Christian communities of Palestine, Syria, and Iraq. They never knew a free existence since the rise of Islam. The remaining 8 percent, the Christians of Lebanon mainly, managed to escape to a large extent the *dhimmi* fate, but they did so at great expense in terms of blood and treasure. The post-9/11 U.S. policy of promoting democracy and freedom in the Middle East gave hope to many native Christians, in particular those of Lebanon who had passed through more than a quarter-century ordeal of persecution and Western neglect. The importance of the Christians of Lebanon for the Christians of the wider region cannot be overstated. They have served historically as beacons of freedom and magnets of attraction for their less fortunate brethren in other Arab lands. They have been the lungs, as it were, through which not only other Arab Christians but anyone in the Arab world with a yearning for a freer life could breathe and receive wafts of ideas and inspirations hailing from the open societies of the West.

Following the recent setbacks of the Iraq war, a clear trend of backtracking on this stated American policy of promoting freedom has begun to emerge, and Christians as well as Muslim moderates are feeling let down as a result. Emigration of Christians has started to pick up again, particularly out of Iraq since the heating up of the insurgency and out of Lebanon following the 34-day war of summer 2006 between Hezbollah and Israel. There are in the Middle East an estimated ten to fifteen million native Christians, but their numbers are steadily dwindling. Committed Christians in the West must care about the fate of these ancient and embattled communities. Regrettably, many fall victims to the fallacious logic of some that since a genuine Christian believer can endure anything in this fallen world and remain true to his or her faith, that therefore a free and secure and prosperous existence is not necessary because such a real Christian can be so under any circumstances no matter the hardships. Would fortunate and secure Western Christians easily exchange their privileged situation to live like some of these beleaguered communities of Middle Eastern Christians? In other words, do not begrudge the Christians of the Middle East a free and prosperous existence on the grounds that authentic Christianity can thrive under any pressures. The pursuit of happiness, including security and prosperity in this life, is not something that is antithetical to the Christian faith. Faith in Christ no doubt arms us against the terrible ravages of a cruel world and the sufferings it inflicts, but such faith does not imply refraining from seeking to improve our lot in this life by warding off actual or potential suffering.

Another important lesson to keep in mind is that these are ancient proud churches with deep roots and rich traditions. Helping native Christians to rediscover these roots and traditions, and to revive and nurture them, is the greatest service you can do for them and for yourselves since these very same roots and traditions lie at the foundation of the faith you share with these communities. Do not

view them as hollow relics of a dead past and therefore as prime
candidates for re-conversion to evangelicalism. If that happens
in some cases voluntarily, then that's fine. But don't let a planned
program of seeking recruits among a struggling community take
the place of aiding that community to find its bearings within its
own traditions, experiencing a spiritual revival on this basis, and
achieving a secure and free existence in its own cultural and spiritual
soil.

Most importantly, Christians in the West should not hitch their
eschatological expectations to any seductive wagon that happens to
be passing and thereby inadvertently place these native Christian
communities by association in mortal danger. One example of this
is that of some Christian Zionists who hold to *extreme* versions of
dispensationalism: those who clearly confuse the ancient Chosen
People of Israel (chosen so that the Messiah, who is Jesus of
Nazareth, would come out of them to save the world, as he has
done) with the contemporary state of Israel. Scripture and the church
teach that Jews who remained Jews after the coming of Jesus the
Messiah have not forfeited God's eternally valid choice, but that
the actual meaning of that same choice after Christ's incarnation,
crucifixion, and resurrection has become a mystery to be revealed
and resolved at the end of time. Political Israel today is not the
same thing theologically as the Jews, God's Chosen People after
the coming of Christ. Such identifications with the state of Israel
have been very damaging to indigenous Christians, who have been
accused by Muslims of being Israeli agents, agents of the imperial
West, and a fifth column in the midst of the House of Islam.
Christians of this extreme dispensationalist persuasion need to be
reprimanded whenever they indulge selfishly in these fantasies to
the detriment of local Middle Eastern Christian communities, and
Western Christians must distance themselves from their excesses
and their confusions of the realms of politics and theology. Avoid
at all costs irresponsible apocalypticism; stop eschatologizing the
daily news headlines as Pat Robertson has done regarding Iraq and
Saddam Hussein. Serious evangelicals need to clean house and rid
their ranks of such dangerous embarrassments.

Wherever you find an oasis of free Christianity in the Middle East
such as the one in Lebanon, nurture and protect it; get politically
involved on its behalf, because its disappearance could spell
historically another 1453—the year Constantinople fell irreversibly

to the invading Ottoman Muslims. If Western governments abandon the pledge to spread democracy, freedom, and hope for the peoples of the Middle East, concerned Christians in the West should pursue that challenge and not allow such a noble pledge to turn into a cruel hoax. Often in evangelical circles one hears talk about the architecture of making an impact on God's behalf, and that is indeed a very lofty spiritual challenge for any Christian to undertake. When it comes to the Christian communities of the Middle East, however, this vital spiritual task must be approached with awe and trepidation. Two guiding principles should be applied at all times: addressing these communities has to be done in complete and sincere humility, and deep respect has to be shown for their traditions and histories (i.e., their peculiar situational and experiential context). Western evangelicals therefore must work *with* the local churches, not in spite of them; they must patiently bear and suffer these tormented churches because they too are of God, though imperfect through sin.

The Challenge of Islamism

Islam is a serious spiritual challenge in the world today, and Islamism, which is the extremist version of that religion, must itself also be taken seriously as a spiritual challenge in its own right. Islamism is not the same as Islam, but the two are not unrelated. Certain readings of the Koran and certain jurisprudential and exegetical traditions in Islam could lead to a rigid and intolerant position taken with respect to non-Muslims, or to moderate Muslims, which is precisely what Islamism has, in essence, done. Often Islamism translates into an active call for a worldwide jihad against the infidels (*kuffar*), as is the case with Al-Qaeda, and this jihad invariably entails violence. The Islamist position allows no room for reconciliation or compromise with the forces of infidelity, namely everyone else, and hence there is no concept of permanent peace, but instead at best a possible temporary truce: Osama bin Laden has offered one to the United States and the West on repeated occasions since September 11, 2001; Hamas offered one to Israel as recently as fall 2006.

For some time now, Islam has been facing multiple challenges from modernity, and one of the outcomes of that confrontation has been a heightened degree of fanaticism in the name of rejecting deleterious features of modernity—this is *one* of the sources of Islamism in our time. This process is expected to continue well into the foreseeable future, and it calls for urgent security measures to be put in place to deal with the adverse side effects emanating from this wrestling match between Islam and modernity. Samuel Huntington, the Harvard professor who coined the term "clash of civilizations," mentions a telling phrase: Islam's bloody borders. This is an astute observation on his part because indeed it is quite arresting to see how the Islamic world is encased in red on the map, meaning that wherever Islam comes in contact with non-Islam blood is to be found. The examples are plentiful: Bosnia, Sudan, Mindanao, Kashmir, Afghanistan, East Timor, Bali, Lebanon, Israel/ Palestine, and more. Why is that? Is it all a matter of a vast external conspiracy against Islam and Muslims by a malicious outside world? In certain cases there may well be elements of this. Or is there something inherent to this creed that makes it difficult for Muslims to coexist peacefully with non-Muslims? Is it therefore both these reasons, or is it something else entirely? Whatever the answer, this is a situation requiring urgent security measures, as stated earlier, side by side with sincere attempts to dispel mutual misperceptions and misunderstandings. But the clearing up of these misunderstandings does not come about automatically or swiftly, and certainly not at religious dialogue conferences, no matter how well intentioned. The pathetic state and history of Islamic moderation, with moderates holding the majority but usually staying silent and feeling intimidated, does not help. "All of us against the fanatic few" makes for a nice slogan with little to encourage practical application.

Take, as an example, the cartoon controversy of last fall when a Danish newspaper printed cartoons of Mohammad. Everyone agrees that blasphemy of any sort is vulgar, tasteless, and provocative. Everyday morning, noon, and night our Lord is maligned in a thousand different ways all over the secular West, and specifically in Hollywood. Christians naturally feel very offended. But they recognize that the freedom to blaspheme is also a part of that sacred human right known as freedom of expression. In Islam all pictorial imagery is forbidden, so in fact there is a double offense here for the Muslim: that Mohammad was depicted at all and that he was depicted degradingly. But to understand the depth of the civilizational clash between Muslims and Christians one need only consider two principal misconceptions that emerged from this cartoon controversy: (1) the demand by enraged Muslims that the Danish government apologize for what happened; and (2) the conclusion that since Christians in the West do not take to the streets to burn and destroy and vent their rage violently when Jesus is insulted, then this means they have lost their faith, or their religion is weak, or they have somehow become religious wimps. The first of these misconceptions suggests the total absence in the Muslim mind of any notion of separation of public and private sectors, or of the sanctity of freedom of expression, or of the need for a free and independent press. The second boils down to crying, "You must defend your Prophet!" as the correct expectation from any believer worthy of the designation. Both of these reactions tell us a great deal about Muslims and Islam and how they project their own peculiar categories and assumptions and misconceptions onto others. They are given here as examples to illustrate the huge chasm that would need to be bridged in order to transform the clash of civilizations to a dialogue of civilizations. A former Muslim who abandoned his faith and goes under the assumed name of Ibn Warraq has rightly stated that if the rest of Europe and the West do not stand up on the side of freedom of speech and support Denmark, the Islamization of Europe will have begun in earnest.

There was a time in the past when the church was coercive on the issue of blasphemy, but that went against its most basic beliefs, and it has since performed the necessary mea culpa and moved on. Performing mea culpa, something Pope John Paul II did much of on behalf of the Roman Catholic Church, is actually a sign of strength not weakness—just fathom Saint Augustine's ecclesiology and the meaning of the two cities in his depiction of the Christian worldview. But herein lies yet another instance of misunderstanding and miscommunication with Islam: Islam regards *all* mea culpas as signs of weakness and error. Islam cannot conceive of itself engaging in any such admission of fault on any level. To do like the Pope and the church, or to let pass unanswered an instance of deliberate abuse of the sacred is for Islam an indication that Christians, and the church in particular, have abdicated responsibility and abandoned their religious values and beliefs and no longer stand up for their most cherished articles of faith by actively defending Jesus—even unto perpetrating violence—when he is ridiculed or attacked. We are still unfortunately a very long way off from seeing the emergence of a Muslim Voltaire, someone from within that religious tradition who would stand up and say, I completely disagree with you, but I will defend to the death your right to say what you believe in.

If these misconceptions and misperceptions divide ordinary Muslims from Christians, one can imagine how much more divides Islamists from Christians. Believing Christians in our age need badly to become better acquainted with the nature of Islam generally and with its more extreme and potentially hostile manifestations like Islamism. Before any dialogue or rosy optimism can be indulged in, knowledge and self-protection are crucial first steps. At the end of the day, Islam needs to be seen as a mélange of neo-Arianism, Docetism, and jumbled references to the Old Testament, the New Testament, and apocryphal non- or deuterocanonical books (mainly those ascribed to Thomas and Barnabas). This means that from a Christian standpoint it is a creed replete with half-truths as well as outright errors. However, one thing Muslims consistently display that Christians could learn from is a complete attitude of submission to, and prostration before, God Almighty—herein lies the secret power of their spirituality, their version of "Thy will be done." We must therefore love the Muslim at all times despite everything.

The Question of Russia

This matter has deliberately been set apart from the earlier consideration of Europe because it seems there is a peculiar problem when it comes to attitudes toward Russia, with potentially adverse implications for Christians. The point is simple, even self-evident, yet largely lost. Russia was totally mishandled by the West following the collapse of communism and the end of the Cold War. A lethal combination of patronizing triumphalism and misplaced proselytizing zeal has characterized American and even Christian attitudes to post-communist Russia. The persistent and unnecessary American encroachment on Russia's "near abroad," to borrow a term from the Cold War lexicon, in places like Georgia, Ukraine, the Baltic states, parts of Central Asia, Azerbaijan, and even Belarus, in the name of spreading democracy and freedom, or expanding NATO/ EU membership, and so on, has been very damaging, especially for Russia's reformers, and has rendered inoperable any possible alliance with Russia.

In fact, non-communist Russia, even if emerging slowly out of a long tradition of authoritarianism, ought to be a natural ally in any looming civilizational confrontation. Huntington may have been insightful with "Islam's bloody borders," but he got it all disastrously wrong on Orthodoxy, Russia, and the Orthodox world in general. Orthodoxy is *not* a world apart from the West on fundamental values and ultimate beliefs, as Huntington portrays.[5] Historically, politically, and temperamentally there are clear and often profound differences, but the Orthodox world must be viewed by Western Christians, whether Catholics or Protestants, as an integral and inseparable part of the overall universal Christian civilization. Believing Christians therefore should reach out to Russia on the deepest levels; they should embrace Russia's Christians and Russia's church with her amazing liturgy and her saints; they should study her traditions and immerse themselves in her rich literary heritage that is very Christian (for example, Dostoevsky); they should acquaint themselves with Russia's fine, simple, sturdy common folk, with the intricate shades of her Orthodoxy, indeed with her soul! Whenever possible, help Russia's own church to revive and stand on her feet and live her traditions and her faith. Pope John Paul II tried, but sadly he could not break down the barriers with the Russian church. He did, however, address the Uniate issue—a sticky one between the Roman Catholic and Russian Orthodox churches. Perhaps Pope Benedict XVI will have greater success in bridging the gap with the Russian church.

Know that Russia is on your side. Believe that and let her feel you do. Again, work with the local church. The same should be true for other parts of Orthodox as well as Catholic Eastern Europe. Poland, for example, which is 95 percent Catholic, was instrumental in bringing down communism. For every confused youthful soul in Poland there are tens of thousands who are spiritually very alive and very active. They belong within the Catholic Church where they are very clearheaded about their spiritual priorities. They should be viewed by evangelicals as partners in evangelism, ready co-laborers in the cause of Christ.

---

5. See Samuel P. Huntington, *The Clash of Civilizations and the Remaking of World Order* (New York: Simon and Schuster, 1996), 139–44, 270–72, and throughout the book wherever Orthodoxy is discussed.

The Culture War at Home

Much has been written about this, including the seminal work by Boston College professor Peter Kreeft, and does not need to be rehashed here.[6] That such a war is raging right in the heart of the West, that it is essential it be fought, and that it is winnable are all axioms this author does not question. The most important clue to the successful waging of this war is to target all those elements in our society that in one way or another promote the culture of death. Required for waging this war is intellectual rigor based first and foremost on the acknowledged harmony between faith and reason, religion and science. One important recent source where the interested Christian might start is Pope John Paul II's encyclical *Fides et Ratio* (faith and reason).

Consider, for example, the debate raging between creationism and evolutionism. The problem is that the entire debate as it is conducted is flawed from the outset, and is largely unnecessary: neither do the so-called creationists represent the only religious position or side of the argument, nor do the evolutionists dispose of religion altogether or of the religious position when they expose the errors and shortcomings of creationism. A proper Augustinian understanding of the way Scripture ought to be read and interpreted would reveal that creation of all that there is by an omnipotent and omniscient God is not necessarily incompatible with Darwin's theory of evolution. This, by the way, is the Catholic Church's position. As for intelligent design, there is nothing new there; it is the old argument for God's existence based on evidence of design updated to accommodate the most recent scientific findings. That is fine, provided we as Christians don't get too hung up on rational or scientific "proofs" and start to substitute them for faith as gift and grace (Augustine again, basing himself on Saint Paul).

In the fog of the battle do not be confused by new names and fads and buzzwords. For example, everything these days seems "post" something: postmodern, post-metaphysical, post-Christian, post-9/11, post-oriental studies, post-feminism, etc. What is this morbid fascination with "moving beyond," this mad rush to declare everything as obsolete? It is a faddish fetish and an obsession with sheer novelty;

6. See Peter Kreeft, *How to Win the Culture War: A Christian Battle Plan for a Society in Crisis* (Downers Grove, IL: InterVarsity, 2002).

it is exasperation with the permanence of truth. It all really began
in modern times with Nietzsche's famous "beyond good and evil,"
namely his attempt to transcend and overturn traditional/conventional
morality. Man is running out of names to describe how he wishes
to scurry ahead of himself (in fact, to run away *from* himself—to
leave himself behind). All this boils down to the morbid urge to deny
the permanent, the durable, the perennial, the unchanging. A good
example of this "time to move on" impulse is Richard Rorty's *The
Future of Religion*[7] where the author "imagines" new ways of what
it is to be religious—a kind of post-recognizable religiosity type of
thing! And since much of the discussion of the culture war, if not the
actual war itself, takes place in the media or at the academy, being
both media savvy and academically adept become musts for those
Christian foot soldiers on the frontlines of the war. The enemy reduces
itself to a variety of Christophobes who don't hesitate to indulge in
the fallacy of moral equivalence and who are basically consumed by
blind hatred for everything smacking of Jesus Christ.

The Ecumenical Imperative

In Lebanon, the home country of this author, an effort was begun
some years ago at Christian teaching for youth from a variety of
Christian denominations. The reason was that the private secular
school attended by many of these youths offered no religious
instruction. Parents needed to find a suitable alternative, so they
devised an interdenominational forum they called Cross Talk, which
remains the only such Christian teaching program that caters
at once to Catholics, Orthodox, and Protestants anywhere. This
biblically-grounded ecumenical effort was ad hoc and informal at
first, with the teaching done by some of the parents themselves, and
it subsequently received the joint official blessings of the respective
local churches involved. Cross Talk now serves young people ages
four to eighteen (some 320 in total) and is looking to acquire new
premises to accommodate its expanding clientele. It is truly the
work of the Holy Spirit in every way!

If the people who set up Cross Talk under the guidance of the
Spirit could do it in little Lebanon, then Christians in America and the

7. Gianni Vattimo, Richard Rorty, and Santiago Zabala, *The Future of Religion* (New York: Columbia University Press, 2005).

West should be able to cooperate much more closely than they have been. Protestants need to be reminded that the Inquisition is over, the indulgences are gone, and the corrupt medieval popes are a thing of the past. If the Catholic Church and the pope are doing the right thing these days, join hands with them. Cooperation against the holocaust of abortion has been an admirable example. More such examples of cooperation are needed. Don't see the pedophile scandal through the prism of the secular media establishment; accept sincere apologies and move on. At all costs avoid schadenfreude; it is unchristian. Be open to churches other than your own. Being a community of believers, Christians were never intended to live only a purely vertical spiritual life—the individual believer, the Book, and God—but a horizontal one as well—a community of the faithful, an ecclesia. And the vertical together with the horizontal form the cross. Thank God for the first one thousand years of Christianity, the first millennium! There was only one church and there were the great church fathers and the early church councils in addition to the canonical Scriptures. It was tough to battle all those heresies and to painstakingly work out those intricate issues in Christology, but the church received constant help from the Holy Spirit. Let us agree at least to concentrate on the common ground we all share from those first thousand years—it is a very rich and redeeming legacy. The more recent antagonisms and prejudices are paralyzing, so avoid or bracket them for the time being.

Conclusion

Being a committed Christian invariably means being so in the midst of turmoil, anxieties, challenges, dangers, and the loss of tranquility. But such Christians are familiar with these situations and are ready for them because they know the meaning of the cross. Our Savior has prepared us for precisely this state of affairs—to be his followers *in the world*. Every age presents its own peculiar assortment of crosses to be endured and overcome. The question that recurs every time is: do we engage, or do we withdraw? But the two are not really contradictory as they might first seem. In fact, a committed Christian is prepared to do both, each at the proper time. Knowing when to engage and plunge into the fray and when to remain on the sidelines preferring to pray and contemplate in serenity and perform occasional concrete and discreet acts of charity—this wise discernment is precisely what the Holy Spirit provides. The book of Revelation clearly intimates to us, however one interprets the symbols, that matters are going to get much worse before they get better. Jesus himself told us people will do this and that to us because of his name's sake, but that he is with us until the end of time. Crises both personal and collective, internal and external, are the order of a fallen world, but rejoice and be glad, he says, for "I have overcome the world!" Clashes of cultures and civilizations is only one type of crisis that tests us and deepens our faith if we embrace the cross and allow the Comforter, sent to us by Jesus and his Father, to take charge of our lives. This then is the true meaning of "love conquers all."

Discussion Questions

1. Of the six civilizational challenges facing Christians today:

   Which one have you encountered the most?

   Which one is of most urgent concern to you?

   Which are you in a position to address or affect?

2. What does it mean to say that Europe has become post-Christian?

3. Why does the spiritual fate of Europe matter for Christians?

4. Why are the Middle East's Christians dwindling in numbers?

5. Why is it important to respect the local traditions of Middle Eastern churches and work with, rather than in spite of, them?

6. What is Islamism and how should it be faced?

7. What is it about Russia that makes it much closer to the West than might appear?

8. What role might you be uniquely qualified to play:

   In the re-evangelization of Europe?

   In nurturing struggling Christian communities in the Middle East?

4

WHERE WOULD WE BE TODAY IF WE TOOK MALIK'S *CHRISTIAN CRITIQUE OF THE UNIVERSITY* TO HEART?

PETER KREEFT

I recently discovered Charles Malik's work, *A Christian Critique of the University*,[1] and was blown away by it. I'm not a fan of talking about how to talk or educating people on how to educate, so I did not expect anything that remarkable in a book on education. But I would say this is the single masterpiece in the twentieth century on Christian education, unless you count C. S. Lewis's *The Abolition of Man*.

Since I am a beginner with regard to Professor Malik, I will use a beginner's method: I will let myself be taught rather than teach. That is, about half of my words are going to be his words, and I will be very content to be a dwarf climbing up on the shoulders of this giant.

---

1. Charles Malik, *A Christian Critique of the University*, 2nd ed. (Ontario: North Waterloo Academic Press, 1987). First edition published Downers Grove, IL: InterVarsity, 1982. All references hereafter will be from the second edition.

Where would we be if we had taken his advice? Nobody knows. Nobody has a crystal ball. But the *necessity* of taking his advice is the burden of this chapter. We have done very little in the way of taking the advice of this great book, so let me try to repeat his message. I have four main points.

First, I will reflect on the importance of the university for Western civilization: its past, present, and future. Second, I will address the meaning and absolute need for asking the question, the main point of the book, "What does Jesus Christ think of the university?"[2] Third, I will consider how that question is going to fall on our universities, which are certainly in crisis. I will discuss the historical fall of universities from their original tasks to their present state and the idolatry and arrogance that Professor Malik sees in the sciences and the humanities. And finally, a solution. I will discuss three specific solutions and one general solution.

Professor Malik insisted on not abandoning secular universities but regenerating them. He also suggested the formation of an ongoing institute to study this problem. He was also strong on the ecumenical dimensions of that problem and the need for an ecumenical solution, not only among Christians but also between Christians and Muslims, which is an area I'd like to explore. Finally, the most important question of all is, what kind of person must you be in order to implement the solution? That is indeed the first question. I love the Chinese saying: "When the wrong man uses the right means, the right means work in the wrong way."

The Importance of the University for Western Civilization

I never realized how important the university was for our civilization until I read this passage from chapter 1 of *A Christian Critique of the University*:

> The university is one of the greatest creations of Western civilization. There is the family, the church, the state, the economic enterprise, the professions, the media, and the university. These seven institutions with all their living traditions and with all that they mean, constitute the substance of Western civilization. And while in other civilizations there are families, religious institutions, states, institutions for the

---

2. Ibid., 24.

creation of goods and wealth, a profusion of crafts and professions
and even certain public modes of disseminating information, the
university, as universally recognized today, is more distinctive of
Western civilization than of any other.[3]

This great Western institution . . . dominates the world today more
than any other institution: more than the church, more than the
government, more than all other institutions. All the leaders of
government are graduates of universities. . . . The same applies to all
church leaders. . . . The professionals—doctors, engineers, lawyers,
etc.—have all passed through the mill of . . . the university. And the
men of the media are university-trained.[4]

It's a simple cause-and-effect principle. Touch the cause and
you touch the effect. Influence the university and you influence
the world.

Our universities are in crisis. They are in crisis partly because
they have not been faithful to their origins. They have a double
origin: secular and religious, Greek and Christian.

The ultimate origin of the university is among the Greeks. Here
is how the Greeks were distinctive, unique:

More than by anything else, Western civilization is *defined* by total
fearlessness of and openness to the truth. To the extent this civilization
begins to harbor reservations about this fearlessness and this openness
it ceases to be itself, i.e., Western; and to the extent a society, any
society, has developed fearlessness of and openness to the truth, it
has become Westernized. . . . An inhibition of [this] original curiosity
has blunted Soviet universities. . . . This blunting, inhibiting virus has
infected Western universities themselves [especially] with respect
to the knowledge of Christianity. . . . The original universal Greek
curiosity is gradually becoming overwhelmed![5]

Notice the togetherness of the secular and the religious here.
The principal of openness to truth is not a distinctively Christian
principle, but on the basis of that principle openness to Christianity
would be a part of the university's program. How much does Harvard
University talk about Christianity in the classroom? So this is not

3. Ibid., 15.
4. Ibid., 19–20.
5. Ibid., 19.

just a lack of fidelity to Christianity, it's a lack of fidelity to itself as a university.

What are at stake in this crisis, he says, are not only the mind and spirit and character of our children. What could be more important than that? When our own mind and spirit and character are at stake, then the entire fate of Western civilization and therewith the fate of the world is at stake as well.

This is not, however, a doomsday scenario. It is an opportunity. A crisis is a means of growth. The glass of water is always half full. Every great achievement in history is a result of a crisis. It's the "challenge and response" that Arnold Toynbee defined as the moving force of human history. The university, Malik writes, is "a clear-cut fulcrum with which to move the world."[6] Remember Archimedes's famous statement: "Give me a lever and a fulcrum to rest it on and I can move the world." What is the Archimedean point of the world today? The university.

The challenge is for the church to realize this: that no greater service can it render both to itself and to the cause of the gospel with which it is entrusted than to try to recapture the universities for Christ, on whom they were all originally founded. That is simply a historical fact. Not only does the university need to pay attention to the church, but the church needs to pay attention to the university. More potently than by any other means, change the university and you change the world. The ministry of the Christian scholars, the ministry of educators, is not somewhere out in left field. It's on the pitcher's mound. It is not an extra; it is perhaps the single most important public social ministry of the church in our age.

Christ and the University

What is the fundamental question about the relation between Christ and the university? Characteristically, Malik did not accept the ordinary answer to that question. When I think of his mind I always think of the mind of G. K. Chesterton. There was one thing that could not find a home in either mind, although it finds many homes in ours, and that one thing is baloney. Fashionable clichés were ruthlessly demolished and stood on their heads. Malik's question is not, "What does the university think of Jesus Christ?"

---

6. Ibid., 100.

His question is, "What does Jesus Christ think of the university?"[7]
C. S. Lewis in *The Weight of Glory* tells of the realization that what
people used to say is wrong. They used to say, "What we think of
God is the most important question." He said, "By God Himself,
it is not! How God thinks of us is not only more important, but
infinitely more important."[8]
What's the standard of truth? How I think of God or how God
thinks of me? What the university thinks of Christ or what Christ
thinks of the university? If I am the standard then Christ is an
object, and if I am the university I am the judge and Christ is in
the dock. It's the other way around. We're in the dock. God says
the words, "I AM" (Ex. 3:14) before we do. That's what it means
to be in his image. It has been said that "God created man in His
own image and we've been returning the compliment to God ever
since."

The foreword to *The Christian Critique of the University* describes
the book as the third of the annual Pascal lectures on Christianity
and the university. In comparing Charles Malik to Pascal, the author
of the foreword, John North, quotes Pascal:

> Not only do we only know God through Jesus Christ, but we only know
> ourselves through Jesus Christ; we only know life and death through
> Jesus Christ. Apart from Jesus Christ we cannot know the meaning
> of our life or of our death, of God or of ourselves.[9]

And those are the only four important things we must know.

Malik writes, "What does Jesus Christ think of the university?"[10]
That is the question. "[The question] is valid and it has an answer.
We may not know the answer but the answer *exists*."[11] It's a nice
way of saying there is objective truth. Truth is not "whatever my
department lets me get away with saying." We may not know the
answer, but the answer exists, and we may expectantly seek it,
for even if it eludes us it is still there. You might think this is too
difficult a question. A much easier question to answer is, what does

7. Ibid., 24.
8. C. S. Lewis, *The Weight of Glory* (San Francisco: Harper Collins, 2001),
38.
9. Malik, *Christian Critique of the University*, 10.
10. Ibid., 24.
11. Ibid.

the university think of Christ? Empirical research can tell you what
the university thinks of Christ. Just send around people with tape
recorders. But despite the fact that the question, what does Christ
think of the university? is more difficult to answer, it's infinitely
more important to answer, and we *can* hope to answer it because
the answer is there.
Malik says:

> We are not thinking of the university first and then as a sort of
> afterthought of Jesus Christ; we are thinking of Jesus Christ first,
> and all along and in his light we see the university.[12]

> I have put [the question] in this form rather than in the fashionably
> more acceptable form: How do we see the university from the Christian
> point of view?, because this way of putting the question soon lands us
> in some form of subjectivism which, as the bane of modern thought,
> is precisely, as we shall see, what is at stake with the university today.
> "From the Christian point of view" has no solid foundation unless
> the word *Christian* here means Jesus Christ himself. So from the very
> start I have put aside all such questionable phraseology as "from the
> Christian point of view," "in terms of Christian principles," "applying
> Christian principles or values," "from the standpoint of Christian
> culture," etc.[13]

Notice how comfortable academics are with abstract phrases
and how uncomfortable they are with concrete words like "Christ."
"In fact," Malik continues, "it is already a concession to entitle this
study *A Christian Critique of the University* rather than simply and
directly *What Does Jesus Christ Think of the University?*"[14]
Now I love InterVarsity Press, but I must criticize them for not
allowing Professor Malik to publish the book under his original
title, which is the real question: what does Jesus Christ think of
the university?
The need for that question is absolute and obvious. That's the
next step:

> If the university today dominates the world, if Jesus Christ is who
> the church and the Bible proclaim him to be, and if we happen to

---

12. Ibid.
13. Ibid., 25.
14. Ibid.

believe that . . . then how can we fail, not only to raise the question
of what Jesus Christ thinks of the university, but to face the equally
urgent demand: What can be done?[15]

We know and love Jesus Christ and that is why we ask the question
and seek his will for the university. Those who do not ask it either
do not know him, or know him but are afraid of him, or hate him,
or do not want to ask it. . . . But it is impossible for one who knows
and loves Jesus Christ not to ask the question and seek, in fear and
trembling, an answer to it.[16]

Notice how Malik focuses you. He doesn't let you take side roads.
This is the highway. This is the main way. This is the central
question. So everything in the book is only about that one central
question.

Jesus is always doing that, too. He seems in the gospels to
sometimes be clever and avoid things. No. It's others who are clever
and avoid things. For instance, the disciples ask him, "Lord, will
many be saved?" And his answer is, "Strive to enter in" (Luke 13:24,
KJV). Well, why doesn't he answer the question directly? Fifty percent
will be saved. Or 10 percent or 90 percent. Surely he knows. He
doesn't answer the question directly because that's not the question.
Those are the words. The real question was the questioner. Jesus has
this incredible way of not being distracted by words. He answered
the questioner. And if we can do that too, we do his work. That's
the *only* way we can do his work, by talking to the real person
inside, not the mask and the tongue and the words that the person
manipulates. Powerful and effective Christians always do that. I
mentioned Pascal, I mentioned Chesterton, and I should mention
St. Augustine. Professor Malik is in that category. Like a hunter he
goes for the jugular:

Our immovable position is that Jesus Christ exists, that he has a will
for everything, especially for that most important thing, the university,
that the question as to his will for the university can and should be
asked, that if we seek it with all our heart and mind and strength, he
will, at his pleasure, reveal it to us.[17]

---

15. Ibid., 21.
16. Ibid., 105.
17. Ibid., 104.

Jesus said, "Seek and you will find" (Matt. 7:7). "And that even if
we do not know or find the answer, *the answer nevertheless is still
there.*"[18]

The university exists and Jesus Christ exists and the future exists,
and the university and the church and our children and grandchildren
and the whole fate of man and civilization are crying for us to do
something. No man can comprehend what is involved here without
burning to do something. This is why I must confess I am a little
skeptical of conferences. Conferences are full of words. Words are
often substitutes for action.

Mother Theresa was at a conference once. She didn't like to
go to conferences. This was an ecumenical conference. She was
interested in ecumenism, so she sat patiently through four or five
long theological talks. They asked her what she thought about them,
and she said, "They talk too much." They said, "But, Mother, these
are academics, these are theologians. They're eloquent. That's what
they do. They talk. What else could they do?" She was in an outdoor
tent and the floor was a bit dirty and there was a broom in the
corner, so she answered the question by pointing to the broom. She
said, "Well, the floor is kind of dirty. One of them could have picked
up that broom and swept the floor. That would have said more." I
think it would have. I don't think anyone remembered any sentence
in any of those talks, but if one of those theologians would have
picked up a broom they would have been talking about that until
Christ came again.

The Crisis of the University

That the university is in crisis should be fairly obvious, but let
us make sure we understand the obvious, and in the correct way.
We see the appearance. We see the empirical facts that we cannot
ignore, but we may not remember the ultimate cause. It's certainly
not fashionable to speak of the ultimate cause. What is the ultimate
cause? Here it is; here is the ultimate meaning of history: we always
have, in the womb of history and in the heart of man, *Christ and
Antichrist* contending. Spiritual warfare is a pervasive theme in
Scripture, present on almost every page. It is an utterly unfashionable
theme to hear today. We hear instead much about "progress."

---

18. Ibid.

"The forces of this kind of progress have as their ultimate aim to obliterate from history the very mention of the Name of Jesus and his cross."[19] I am told that in the nation my four grandparents were born in, the Netherlands, it will soon be illegal to mention the name Jesus in public schools.

> Inquire diligently what the word *progressive* means (progressive person, progressive doctrine, progressive law, progressive attitude, progressive system, progressive tendency, progressive movement, progressive society, progressive culture, progressive country), and you will find it for the most part directed, consciously or unconsciously, against Jesus Christ. There is always something else put forward to make us forget him: justice, science, culture, prosperity, pleasure, serenity, peace. The important thing is to replace him . . . to crowd him out of existence altogether. Jesus radically disturbs. . . .[20]

There should be no controversy at all about whether you have to be countercultural. By definition Jesus is always countercultural, and when that is forgotten corruption always sets in. "Jesus radically disturbs, and the disturbance must once and for all be put to rest."[21]

We know that the first universities, which set a pattern for all other universities, were founded on Jesus Christ. Every single Ivy League university was, for instance, once a "Christian" university. Harvard still has as its motto, "Truth for Christ and the Church." And we know that that foundation has now in practice become a relic of the past. *A Christian Critique of the University* raises the question of why this has happened. Is it a natural phenomenon? No. Was it an inevitable development? No. What were the ultimate spiritual causes behind it? The devil. Does it really signify progress? Well, if advanced tooth decay is progress, then yes. Progress from what to what? From childhood to adulthood? Remember how the term "adult" is used in modern America. What is an adult bookstore or adult movie?

"Can the university be recaptured for Christ? . . . Who is going to win, Christ or Antichrist?"[22] Those are two different questions.

---

19. Ibid., 31.
20. Ibid.
21. Ibid.
22. Ibid., 32.

The answer to the first question is yes. The answer to the second question ultimately is Christ, but Antichrist can win a lot of territory and a lot of souls temporarily. Yes, the gates of hell do not prevail against the church (cf. Matt. 16:18), but unfortunately they can prevail against many of her members.

Professor Malik analyzes the crisis in the two basic parts of the university, the sciences and the humanities. He gets specific and embarrassing, and therefore very useful. First, the sciences:

> More serious is what happens to the scientist himself. . . . First is what I call the pride of knowledge and power. . . . Because he controls his subject matter, the scientist slips into the feeling that he is a kind of god. People speak of the humility of the scientist; in truth I find very little humility among scientists. They know, it is true; but what they do not know is not only greater but far more important than what they know. They control, it is true; but they are controlled far more than they control.[23]

It's the old master/slave relationship. Does it matter if your slaves are made of flesh or if they're made of metal or silicon or fiber optics? In each case, the slave is free and the master is enslaved to his need for the slave, but the slave has no need for the master. So though externally the master controls the slave, internally that is not so. Internally the master's own need for the slave controls the master. It's all in the Lord of the Rings. What do they teach them in school nowadays, anyway?

We return to Malik:

> Second is what I call the illicit transfer of authority. Many scientists think . . . that their recognized competence in their own field qualifies them to pass judgment on matters pertaining to other spheres . . . questions of man, morals, philosophy, theology, history, truth, freedom, destiny, trial, suffering, God, Christ, the Spirit, the church. . . . Scientists should humbly acknowledge that there are authorities in other fields too, and should seek them and sit at their feet. . . .[24]

> Third is the error of naturalism. Because scientists give themselves to nature all their lives they often end up by worshiping it.[25]

---

23. Ibid., 42.
24. Ibid., 42–43.
25. Ibid., 44.

Fourth, the scientist, wrapped up in and dedicated to nature, forgets himself. The fact that he is "human," in that he suffers, loses his temper, is tempted, often falls, is selfish, is terribly limited, envies, resents, schemes, hates, is caught up in frenzied rivalries with his colleagues, rejoices in the misfortunes of others, is in desperate need for fellowship and love, faces death any minute, often does not stand up for truth and justice, often lends a hand to slander, often is not fair in his judgment of others, often wishes others did not exist and therefore murders them in his thought—all these common human frailties he is as much heir to as any other person. Science cannot save the scientist from them. In fact, like other people, scientists are prone to flee from them.[26]

Wonderfully ruthless honesty, isn't it?

A "Christian" critique of the university is concerned with this fourfold temptation of the scientist—pride, pretending to know what he does not know, naturalism and self-forgetting—because Jesus Christ judges the scientist on the basis of these temptations even more than on the excellence of his scientific achievements.[27]

You think that's bad? Wait until you get to the humanities!

When I started teaching back in the early 1960s, most of the atheists were science majors. Now most of the science majors are theists and most of the atheists are English majors. English and history are probably the two most corrupt departments. If the humanities were themselves in a healthy state from the point of view of Jesus Christ, they would provide the necessary corrective to the problem of the sciences, but they are not.

What's missing? And what's present? Well, what is present is usually *presupposed*:

What is presupposed is often far more subtle and potent than what is explicitly taught; what you are silent about will pass as something so much taken for granted that you do not need to say a word about it; while what you explicitly put forward may be arguable. Therefore seek first what the university is silent about, and then you know the secret of the university.[28]

---

26. Ibid., 44–45.
27. Ibid., 45.
28. Ibid., 70.

[T]here is something almost universally absent in all the humanities, and that is any reference to something genuinely transcendent. . . .[29]

Malik lists a few dozen problems in the humanities, but I'm going to focus on just four. One is skepticism:

Nothing certain. No absolute. All ultimately misty. Living in a world of doubt and suspicion. Every sentence hedged by some reservation, some warning, some caveat.[30]

Otherwise you're dogmatic, simpleminded. Two and two may be four if you really believe it. Even deeper is cynicism:

There is also a great deal of cleverness, calculation and cynicism in the humanities. . . . One seeks in vain for the great and confident mind that takes a firm and sustained stand on the great issues of life and death and purpose and meaning and being. . . . In business and in the technological world one finds such minds, and in their own spheres they are respected, but very rarely in the realm of the humanities. What meets us here is for the most part the chilling smile of the cynic . . . who dismisses everything, even the most momentous . . . who enjoys the game of elaborating endless arguments which invariably end up in the total obfuscation of what is discussed. Darkness, uncertainty, insecurity, the dissolution of being into non-being, the "vanity of vanities, all is vanity" of Ecclesiastes—this is the mood and fundamental attitude. . . . The lips are not firm, there is not even laughter: there is only that soul-scorching awful smile.[31]

Those of you who teach in humanities departments in secular universities unfortunately know what Malik means. Still deeper, nihilism:

It is incredible how much the spirit of nihilism pervades the humanities today. . . . Pull down and annihilate everything that is: customs, traditions, institutions, establishments, revered values, the sensibilities of parents, the names of the great, the classical norms. The rule, the intent, is to debunk everything. And while you are not in power yourself, pull down those who are. The spirit of destroying everything

---

29. Ibid., 71.
30. Ibid., 73.
31. Ibid., 77–78.

stalks the earth. The malicious pleasure in destruction is one of the most deep-seated impulses in human nature: it is Satanic.[32]

Even Freud came close to recognizing that. It's a death wish.

One more characteristic of the humanities is an index of their decadence. It is something very specific, very concrete, very apparently small but much more telling than we think. Everyone is in a hurry. Our relationship to *time* is about the same as our relationship to nature; we have to conquer it. "The humanities, both students and professors, are in a hurry. They must get somewhere! God knows where!"[33] This is your pilot speaking. We have good news and bad news. The good news is we are proceeding at 750 miles per hour. The bad news is we have no idea where we're going.

"They cannot rest where they are! 'Be still and know that I am God,' that they hardly know. Stillness, which belongs to the essence of the humanities, has been distilled out of them altogether."[34] One insight that keeps haunting me from Kierkegaard, repeated constantly in the *Journals* goes something like this: "If I could prescribe one remedy for all the ills of the modern world I would prescribe silence. For even if the truth were proclaimed, even if the word of God were proclaimed from the housetops it would not be heard. There is too much noise. So first create silence."

But, Malik writes:

> The deadline must be met, the manuscript must be completed, the dissertation must be revised, the meeting must be attended, the appointment must be kept, the news must be followed, the developments must be watched, the latest literature must be mastered, their anxieties about their position and their future must be allayed—and therefore they can give you only five minutes! And even in these five minutes their mind is not on you. There is no stillness, no quiet, no rest, no living in the presence of eternity, no overcoming of time and its pressures, no unfretting patience, no resting in being just yourself. . . . They must be on the go all the time. Again, on the go where—God knows.[35]

[T]he humanities mean peace, grace, patience, communion with others, the joys of fellowship and sharing, the art of relaxed, creative

---

32. Ibid., 78.
33. Ibid., 80.
34. Ibid.
35. Ibid.

conversation, abiding friendship, love—love of the subject matter and love of your friends—the suspension of time, forgetting even yourself, that incredible inner-freedom which creates on the spot, God knows how and God knows from where.[36]

It's the secret of creativity. It seems that that's the thing the humanities are terrified of.

One of the things I am most impressed by in this analysis is that Malik does not simply talk like a sociologist and give you statistics, facts, problems, the obvious surface data. He goes to *causes*. And they are not just the causes that we all know. He goes deeper into very concrete things, very specific things. And therefore his solutions are also very concrete and very specific.

The Solution for the University

Malik gives us a four-aspect solution. Aspect number one is strategy. Should we start new universities, or should we try to save the old ones? There are some very good new universities arising. Is that an adequate answer? He doesn't think it is:

[S]hall we concentrate on recapturing the great established universities for Jesus Christ or, despairing of this task, shall we choose the line of least resistance and concentrate on establishing new Christian universities to compete with them? . . . If we concentrate only on competing, two problems arise. First, the established institutions started centuries ago with as sincere an intention as ours to serve Jesus Christ; and so how do we know that we will succeed in holding out against the onslaught of secularism, rationalism, relativism, humanism, immanentism, etc., more than they did? . . . Second, can we really compete if we start, comparatively, virtually from scratch?[37]

If the boat is sinking, do you take the life boat and abandon the Titanic? No, you rescue all the passengers you can. I don't think it's an either/or. You do both.

The second specific recommendation, the point and conclusion of the whole book, is reminiscent of Martin Luther King Jr.'s "I Have a Dream" speech:

36. Ibid., 81.
37. Ibid., 106.

Let us now think of a different procedure I spoke of as a dream. But let us give this dream a name; let us call it "The Institute." I do not like the term *institute* because there are numerous and sundry institutes around, and we have in mind a task much more important, more far-reaching and more historically decisive than the task of any existing institute.[38]

The mandate of this Institute is fourfold: (a) To find out, in the most authoritatively objective manner possible, the exact state of mind, morals and spirit in the universities. . . . (b) To let, in fear and trembling, Jesus Christ judge this existing state of mind, morals and spirit. . . . (c) To consider the possibility of bringing Christ back to the university and to suggest practical ways and means to that end. (d) To consider that its mandate shall last as long as there are universities, namely, indefinitely.[39]

Astonishingly, Malik then points out that no government, no foundation, no university, and even no church has ever set up such a corporate body. Why? The book's been out. We have read it and talked about it. We have agreed. Why haven't we done it? Because it's much easier to talk about something than to do it, and it's wonderful being an academic: you can actually persuade yourself that you've done something simply because you've thought about it and talked about it. That's how important thought is to you.

That sounds insane, but academics, as a class, are closer to insanity than anyone else. We have a saying in academia: "That idea is so crazy you have to have a PhD to believe it." In 1900 there were one hundred times more farmers than PhDs. In the year 2000 there were one hundred times more PhDs than farmers. That says a lot about why you can fool people today.

Here is the third aspect of Malik's solution. He doesn't give it a name. I'll give it a name. I'll call it "chutzpah" or "moxie." He contrasts the Christian response with the Muslim response, or at least a typical Christian response with a more typical Muslim response. And here I think we have something very much to learn from the Muslims. He writes:

A couple of years ago a Muslim Pakistani won a Nobel award in physics. Many other people were also honored with Nobel prizes

38. Ibid., 110.
39. Ibid., 112.

for their diverse accomplishments. The press interviewed most of
them about their reactions to the awards when they first heard of
them. With the exception of the Pakistani, they all said that they
were overjoyed, that they celebrated with their families and friends,
and they expressed the normal feelings of satisfaction that people
experience on such occasions. Only the Pakistani said that his first
act was to pray to Allah (God) and thank him for having illuminated
his mind and enabled it to penetrate some of the mysteries of his
creation. . . . The Muslim scientist first thought of Allah (God) and
not of himself or of science or of truth or of nature or of his own
achievement. The Christian scientists . . . can emulate the Muslims
in their total fidelity to their faith and in the courage with which they
confess it from the housetops.[40]

I had a Muslim student in a comparative religion class once at
Boston College, about twenty years ago. It was a class of about
twenty-four students. Most of them were Catholic, and there was a
Muslim and a Jew sitting in the front row. They were the two best
students. They were fighting all the time about Palestine and they
were fighting me all the time, and I loved it. They asked the hard
questions. During the break (it was a three and a half hour class
so we had a long break), we often had better discussions than in
the class. One day we were sitting munching on potato chips and
drinking Coke when the Jewish student pointed behind my head
at the cinder block wall and said, "Is that supposed to be a cross?"
I turned and noticed that it looked like a faint cross was painted
there, and I realized that that's where the crucifix used to be. Boston
College had taken it down.

So I turned around and with an embarrassed smile opened my
mouth to make some lame excuse, and the Holy Spirit shut my
mouth and opened the mouth of a Catholic student next to him who
said, "Oh no, we used to have crucifixes but we took them down." And
the Jewish student said, "When?" (Why is he asking when instead
of why?) The student said, "Last semester, I think." And the Jewish
student said, "Aha! The Bundy money!" He explained that when
President Carter assumed office there was a case that was about
to go to the Supreme Court, and it was going to be very divisive.
Can federal money to go parochial schools without violating the
separation of church and state? McGeorge Bundy had brokered a

40. Ibid., 55.

deal under a previous administration so that the answer was yes, if and only if the school was not sectarian or negative or "narrow." It was vague enough to satisfy everybody.

The Jewish student pointed out that in the semester following that decision, in order to apply the Bundy decision, all twenty-one Jesuit colleges in America took down their crucifixes. The Catholic student was rather abashed and said, "We wouldn't do that for money." And the Jewish student said, "Of course not. But I hope you got more than thirty pieces of silver this time." Unfortunately, some of the students were so biblically illiterate that he had to explain that Judas Iscariot was the first Catholic bishop to accept a government grant. Then the Catholic student said, "No, we took down the crucifixes to be *ecumenical*."

Then the Muslim student chimed in, "Excuse me, what is the meaning of that word? I do not know 'ecumenical.' " Once again I opened my mouth to answer and once again the Holy Spirit, in the nick of time, shut it and opened the mouth of another student next to him who gave about the stupidest answer to the question imaginable: "Ecumenical means we didn't want to offend anyone else, since we're all equal."

The Muslim student said, "Oh, you did it in order to avoid offending others? You mean like me, the Muslim, and my friend the Jew?" Everyone was very quiet. Those two words were too concrete: "Muslim," "Jew"; we don't talk that language. "People of faith," something vague. "Well, yes," said the Catholic, "we did it so as not to offend you."

"Well you have offended me."

"Why have we offended you?"

"You have called me a bigot."

"No, no, we hate bigotry. That's why we're doing this. Why are you offended by our gesture to you for your sake?"

"Let me try to explain. If you came to my country and enrolled in a Muslim university, you would know you are in a Muslim university. We do not have images, we think it's idolatrous, but you know you are in a Muslim university. Would you be offended at a Muslim symbol in a Muslim university? Of course not. Only a bigot would. Now you expect me to be offended at a Catholic university by a Catholic symbol. So you're calling me a bigot by taking down your crucifixes. I am highly insulted."

I was the only one smiling. I'm a philosopher. I like to smell the wood burning. I like to smell people thinking. Too often the wheel continues turning even after the hamster is dead.

Then, God bless him, the Muslim student turned around like an evangelist, faced the class, and said, "How many of you believe that Jesus is the Son of God?" I said to myself, *Why wasn't I courageous enough to ask that question?* They almost all raised their hand. And he said, "Well we Muslims don't believe that. We think it's an absurd idea. That's pagan. That's idolatry. But we respect Jesus, blessed be his name, as one of the greatest prophets of all time, and we believe that Allah created him without a mother, miraculously, and that he performed miracles and raised the dead and that he is a true prophet and even that he will come again at the end of the world to execute Allah's judgment. So we have a great devotion to Jesus and his mother Mary. Blessed be their names. So if we had pictures of them we would never take them down. Not for any money at all. In fact, if some troops from the government came into our classroom with rifles and fixed bayonets and said, 'There has been a regime change. The law says you must take down the pictures of the prophet Jesus,' then every good Muslim would get out of his chair, go to the front of that picture and say, 'You take down the pictures of our beloved prophet over our dead bodies.' We would be privileged to be a martyr for our beloved prophet. And now you have taken down your pictures of your prophet just to avoid offending us. I think we are better Christians than you." Something deeper than thought was touched that day in my students' souls.

You know, at Georgetown they got the crucifixes back only because the students pressured the faculty and the administration. And the two faculty members that were on the side of the students and organized the thing were a Jew and a Muslim. Why do we have to let others fight our battles for us? That was a typical Muslim response. Here is, unfortunately, a typical Christian response. I speak as a Catholic because I know that place the best. Here is an unfortunate Catholic example: I was on the campus of Notre Dame and was impressed by the students. They are very pious, serious, and holy; they go to church all the time. But the administration is another matter.

This is by Father Richard John Neuhaus from *First Things* magazine:

Many were cheered when Father John Jenkins was appointed president of the University of Notre Dame. I have written in these pages on the recent and encouraging signs that Notre Dame was being renewed in a vibrant sense of its identity and mission as a Catholic University. In January, Fr. Jenkins took up the question of the performance of *The Vagina Monologues* and the sponsorship of a Queer Film Festival as an occasion to address what it means to be a Catholic university. In that statement, he asked many of the right questions and lifted the hopes of those who believe that clear Catholic commitment is the key to Notre Dame's greatness as a university. Then [a few months later] after extensive consultation with faculty, students, and other interested parties, Fr. Jenkins issued his decision. *The Vagina Monologues* and the film festival would continue. This was met with cries of disappointment and outrage from those whose hopes had been lifted. My initial response was to urge calm. While he had made the wrong decision about a potty-mouthed play and a specific promotion of the homosexual cause, I wrote, this does not necessarily define his leadership of Notre Dame. . . . I am afraid I was wrong. Fr. Jenkins himself made the controversy over these two issues a litmus test in defining his understanding of what it means to be a Catholic university. . . . [He] offered the assurance that Notre Dame will try to "achieve balance, to achieve the kind of conversation that is fair, that is intellectually serious, that includes, when appropriate, the Catholic perspective." A university that includes, when deemed appropriate, the Catholic perspective is something less than a Catholic university.[41]

More impressive than Father Jenkins words was the open letter issued by the chairman of the Department of Theology at Notre Dame who noted that

there is "a missing conversation partner. The statement of our president barely mentions the Church . . . [but] whether we recognize it or not this relationship to the Church, to the real, incarnate Body of Christ, the Church as it is with all its blemishes and not the abstract, idealized Church in our minds—is the lifeblood and only guarantee of our identity as a Catholic university. There is no Catholic identity apart from affiliation with the Church. . . . The ancient Gnostic heresy developed an elitist intellectual tradition which eschewed connection to the "fleshly" church of the bishop. . . . Are we in danger of developing

41. Richard John Neuhaus, "While We're at It," *First Things* 164 (June/July 2006): 63–64.

a gnosticized version of the "Catholic intellectual tradition," one which floats free of any norming connection and so free of any concrete claim to Catholic identity?[42]

At the very least the Bible provides a kind of "church on paper" for all Protestants, even para-church Protestants. But something concrete, some bunch of people, some authority structure must be there as a reference point. Otherwise you have ideas, clouds. Then your thought is like a plane and not a car. Cars can crack up. There are curbs and there are trees. My son as a teenager cracked up the car three times. He is now a pilot. There are no curbs in the air. Academics often forget that thoughts are like cars, they are not like planes, and other thoughts are like curbs. They bump up against them. They contradict them. Above all, things are like curbs. Real things limit and measure thoughts, not the other way around. Thoughts are like cars or curbs. They are not like clouds. Ideas have consequences.

Professor Malik has written some wonderful things. The best thing I have ever read from him is a book called *The Wonder of Being*. It answers the fundamental question, "What kind of a person must you be in order to bring Christ into the university and in order to do His will for the university?" Listen to a few paragraphs from this remarkable work:

> There goes on in the soul of each one of us a fateful struggle between two persons—the person of being and the person of non-being. Which has the upper hand is the deepest question that can be asked about us at any given moment. The person of being stands in awe before the wonderful plenitude of being. . . . The person of non-being dissolves this plenitude. . . . The person of being affirms—and rejoices—in every positive being. The person of not-being . . . only affirms in order to contradict—that is, to destroy some positive being. The person of being sometimes stops talking altogether, because he is lost in contemplation and wonder. The person of not being never stops talking, because that is his way of destroying or suspending or covering up or drowning his sense of amazement at being. . . .
>
> The person of being is always taken by the norm, the rule, that which for the most part is the case; he never averts his gaze from it to the abnormal and exceptional. On the contrary, he understands these only in terms of it. The person of not being appears not to be

42. Ibid., 64.

interested in what is true as a rule, but always hunts the abnormal,
the aberrant, the exotic, and in terms of these he feigns to understand
the rule and the norm. He does not see the wonder of being true as
a norm to be aspired to or as a rule to be upheld. . . . And since there
is no rule to the abnormal, he is always essentially without a rule
himself. . . .

Put a being before a person of being and [he will submit to its
being in love and adoration]. . . . Put a being before the person of
not being, and his first impulse is to manipulate it, to use it, to bring
it under his control; he wants *it* to submit to him.[43]

The single most illuminating sentence I have ever read about the
difference between modern civilization and pre-modern civilization
is found C. S. Lewis's *The Abolition of Man*. He says, "For the wise
men of old the cardinal problem had been how to conform the soul
to reality, and the solution had been knowledge, self-discipline, and
virtue. For [modern man] the problem is how to subdue reality to
the wishes of men: the solution is technique."[44]

The person of being rejoices in being and is deeply thankful for it.
The person of non-being is incapable of thanking or being thankful
for anything. Father Norris Clark, the great Thomist philosopher,
came to Boston College recently and told us of his trip to Tibet. He
went to Tibet on his own to talk with some Buddhist monks on a
very high level. He was at first very impressed by their peace, their
seriousness, their silence, their control of thought and desire. He
asked them, "What ordinary state of mind is the most important
one for what you call the religious life?" and they said, "Gratitude."
And he said, "Wonderful. That is what I would say too. Gratitude for
what?" And they said, "Gratitude for everything." And he said, "That
is extremely wise. Now, to whom are you grateful for everything
if you do not believe in God?" And he said they were incredibly
confused. They said, "We never ask that question." At least they
have the first step; they have gratitude, although they don't know
to whom to be grateful. I think it's far easier to make a Buddhist
into a Christian than to make a deconstructionist into a Buddhist.
Malik continues:

---

43. Charles Malik, *The Wonder of Being* (Waco, TX: Word Books, 1974). The
text cited here is from Charles Malik, "The Wonder of Being," in Kelly Monroe
ed., *Finding God at Harvard* (Downers Grove, IL: Intervarsity, 2007), 338–39.

44. C. S. Lewis, *The Abolition of Man*, 2001 ed. (San Francisco, CA: Harper
Collins, 2001), 77.

The typical act of a person of being is stillness and adoration, as with Jesus' friend Mary. The typical act of a person of not being is business and activity and analytical obfuscation, as with her sister Martha. . . . What is it that calls forth the person of not being in us, and what is it that calls forth the person of being? . . . My answer is that only Jesus Christ of Nazareth calls forth the person of being in us, whether or not we know it. I know why he does it—he does it because he loves us—but I do not know how. . . .

In his tremendous speculations about the teleology of the universe, Aristotle was really seeking Jesus of Nazareth. . . . In his insistence on a supreme and beneficent "good" behind all phenomena . . . Plato was really seeking Jesus of Nazareth. . . . In his wonder about the [mind] behind the order of the universe, Anaxagoras was really seeking Jesus of Nazareth. . . . Do you think it is only in these latter days that people are demythologizing the data of our faith, or romanticizing or secularizing them or denying or explaining them away? There is nothing new in these attempts. The church has faced similar movements in its first seven centuries and dealt decisively with them; we need to restore in our thinking the historical dimension of our heritage. . . . [The only thing that] is really new, radically new, is the new creature in Jesus Christ. . . . How you and I confront and react to Jesus Christ—that is the only really new thing that occurs in history. . . .

Only the new creature, born from above, "born of the Spirit," can see everything in Jesus Christ and Jesus Christ in everything. And only this new birth and this mode of seeing in and through Jesus Christ is new in history. [So] if you take him at his word, then nothing can be the same again for you in the world and in your life.[45]

You would expect that a book that raises questions as serious as these would give a method, a set of answers or guidelines, a way to bring about the will of Christ in the university. The first time I read *The Wonder of Being*, I confess I was disappointed that he didn't do that. Then I realized that this is one of the things that make it a great book. It's like the book of Job. The first few times I read the book of Job I was disappointed. God didn't give Job a philosophical answer. He didn't even read him chapter 1: "See, this is why I'm doing it, I'm testing you." All he said was, "Here I am" (cf. Job 38–40). And Job fell down at his feet and said, "I have heard of thee by the hearing of the ear: but now mine eye seeth thee. Wherefore I abhor myself, and repent in dust and ashes" (Job 42:5–6, KJV).

---

45. Malik, "The Wonder of Being," 340–46.

If Professor Malik had given us a five-year plan or a twelve-step program or a twenty-point manifesto we would have said, "Oh that's the answer." And then we could have prayed, "Jesus, please be the key to open the door to this manifesto or this five-year plan." We would have seen Jesus as the key, and we would have seen the problem as the door. That's the way we usually see our lives. Here we are, and here is our life with all its problems, and here is Christ at the top who has the golden key that will open all the doors. That, I suggest, is *not* the right way to see our lives. Our lives are not an encounter of three things: you, your life, and Christ. Your life is a bi-polar relationship. It's like a ladder. It has a top and a bottom. Think of Jacob's ladder moving between heaven and earth. Here you are at the bottom. Here is Christ at the top. He sends his angels down and up. The ladder is a highway. Everything that happens in your life—your problems, solutions, joys, pain, suffering, your prayers, works, problems of the university, your career, the solutions—these are all tasks sent to you by Christ. Everything is a means to him. Everything is relative to him.

There are only two absolutes because there are only two persons that you will never, ever be able to avoid and escape in all eternity: yourself and Christ. And therefore an answer to the question, how do we do it, valid as that might be, is a temptation to make that the end and Christ a means to it. If, on the other hand, we recognize that Christ is the absolute and that the very problems that we're here worrying about are problems that he has sent to us to be our task, then we think, *Isn't it good that he has put me in these corrupt universities that are so shameless and so empty and so confused, rather than in a fulfilling, wonderful, enthusiastic time and place like the University of Paris in the thirteenth century. Isn't it wonderful?* Yes it is. That's your task. That's your identity. He forges your identity through these things, and he forges the identity of our civilization through these things.

The first answer to what we can do to save the university and to save Western civilization, wonderful and precious as these things are, is to stop idolizing them. We are not guaranteed success and salvation for anything other than our souls. The mind is the captain of the soul. If we capture our thoughts we capture everything else. So thought is absolutely crucial. But neither America nor Greek philosophy nor Western civilization has ever been promised that the gates of hell will not prevail against them. We ourselves are the recipients of that promise. Christ, in his respect for our freedom, has given us the task, "Go and do this but I'm not telling you how. Create the ways." That is what we must do. That is what Charles Malik did.

Where would we be if we had done it, if we had taken Malik's
Christian Critique of the University to heart? We would not be asking
that question in the subjunctive mood; we would be where Christ
wants us to be. Where is that? The only way to find out is to go there, by doing it.

Discussion Questions

1. What difference does it make in trying to "recapture the universities for Christ" that the university has a distinctly Christian
   origin?

2. Why is the question, what does Christ think of the university,
   the truly important question to ask?

3. Empirically it is relatively less difficult to discern what the
   university thinks of Christ. How might we go about discerning
   what Christ thinks of the university? What implications does
   this question have for our own actions with regard to higher
   education?

4. Have you ever witnessed a specific way in which a scientist has
   given in to one aspect of the "fourfold temptation"? Which of
   these four temptations do you believe is most prevalent? How
   is Jesus Christ a response to these temptations?

5. Have you ever witnessed a specific way in which a scholar of
   the humanities has exhibited skepticism, cynicism, or nihilism?
   Which of these three beliefs is most prevalent? What does the
   truth of Christ have to say to each?

6. In what ways do you see "hurry" affecting your own work
   within the university? How do you see it affecting the university as a whole? In what ways can you begin to find peace and
   stillness before God in your daily life? How can you encourage
   others to do the same?

7. Among the various solutions that Malik mentions, which do
   you believe would be most effective? Which do you believe
   would be most practical? Do Malik's solutions generate any
   ideas of your own?

8. How is the "person of being" the necessary antidote for what ails
   the university today? How can one become such a person?

5

ON BEING A CHRISTIAN PROFESSOR IN THE SECULAR ACADEMY

WALTER L. BRADLEY

I attended the University of Texas from 1961 to 1968, earning a BS in Engineering Science (Physics) and a PhD in Materials Science and Engineering. In the seventy-five classes that I took at UT, I never met a Christian professor, though I met many who were not Christians and some who took the opportunity to ridicule the Christian faith I had embraced as a teenager. I wondered during this critical period of my life whether there was something fundamentally incompatible between education to the level of a PhD and Christian faith. Happily, I met (through their books) a profoundly Christian professor from Cambridge University named C. S. Lewis and a Christian thinker named Francis Schaeffer. These authors opened my spiritual eyes, helping me to see a grand Christian worldview, sustained by the God of the Bible who wants to redeem every aspect of his creation, to be Lord over all.

My goal in going to graduate school was to be president of a large technical company, so I took MBA classes along with my engineering classes to prepare. As I began my final year in graduate school at UT, God began to draw me toward a career in the academy. I wondered during this time if it was even possible to be a Christian professor publicly, having seen no role models of what a Christian professor might be and do. But God continued to give me a longing to be for my students what no professor had ever been for me. I had almost been swept away by the intellectual tsunamis of naturalism and secularism during my undergraduate years. I wanted to be the lighthouse for my students that I had never had, helping them avoid shipwreck in the storms that college life surely brings. And so I decided to try the academy as a two-year experiment, accepting a position as a tenure-track assistant professor of metallurgical engineering at the prestigious Colorado School of Mines. I resolved to be easily identified as a Christian professor to my students and colleagues, recognizing that this might get me fired. However, if I could not be an openly Christian professor, then I was happy to return to my original plans to work in industry.

I did not get fired! In fact I got a teaching award my first year, along with research funding from the National Science Foundation, and was tenured after my third year, two years early. I have seen God's faithfulness (1 Thess. 5:18) in guiding and directing me through thirty-eight wonderful years as a Christian professor and would like to share with you the highlights of what God has taught me on this journey.

I will first share biblical principles that I have found to be especially important on my journey in the academy. Then I would like to share practical ways I have found to minister to my students and colleagues. Finally, I would like to address "the outrageous idea of Christian scholarship," a phrase first coined by George Marsden.

Biblical Principles for Christian Academics

This is a very abbreviated list of biblical principles that I have found to be foundational to my journey as a Christian academic. Please excuse my stylizing some of them to read in the way that they might have been written if the intended audience had been exclusively Christian professors.

- *Godspell*: "To see Thee more clearly, to love Thee more dearly, to follow Thee more nearly day by day." This theme song from the famous Broadway play captures the essence of a relationship with Christ. I have found it impossible to have the courage or wisdom to follow Christ in the academy apart from striving to practice the three action verbs—seeing, loving, and following Christ.

- *"Let your light so shine before your students and colleagues, that they may see your good deeds and glorify your Father in heaven"* (Matt. 5:16). St. Francis of Assisi said, "Preach the gospel always and if necessary, use words." But, living a life that exemplifies Christian love and compassion is necessary but not sufficient. I want my students to know that the good things that I do are a result of God's light as it shines through my life. The "necessary words" here are that in some appropriate way I want my students to know that I am a Christian and happy to share more about why with them if they are interested.

- *"Serve wholeheartedly, as if you were serving the Lord, not your department head"* (Eph. 6:7). While I want my life and my work to be pleasing to my department head, my first priority is to spend my time in ways that are pleasing to God, and my department head's priorities do not always align with God's priorities for me.

- *"Whatever you do, work at it with all your heart, as if you are working for the Lord, not for your dean"* (Col. 3:23). I find great motivation in seeing each day as a whole series of opportunities to fulfill God's purposes for me, but I must be listening to let God's voice trump the many conflicting voices that make demands on my time.

- *"No matter how much you publish, you are going to perish anyway, so get over it!"* (Bradley 1:1). Obviously, this did not make the cut when the Bible was put together, but I think it applies anyway, so take it for what you think it is worth.

- *"Seek first his kingdom and his righteousness, and all these things will be given to you as well"* (Matt. 6:33). At many points in my career, I felt the press of a profession that is very, very demanding of my time—tempting me to neglect my family and the Christian ministries to which God has called me. I have repeatedly found God faithful to his promise when I seek him first and don't just give the time that is "left over," which is usually not much.

- *"Let us professors not give up meeting together, as some are in the habit of doing, but let us encourage one another—and*

all the more as you see the Day approaching" (Heb. 10:25). Christian professors need a support system of other professors who understand their challenges and share their same struggles. Christian professors in the secular academy must proactively seek out Christian colleagues with whom they can meet regularly.

- *"Professors who sow sparingly reap sparingly, and professors who sow abundantly reap abundantly"* (2 Cor. 9:6). There are many ways to sow spiritual seeds with your students and colleagues. With one hundred or more new students each semester, Christian professors are uniquely placed to make a spiritual difference in the lives of their students. We should see each student as being in our class by divine appointment, wherever they may be in the spiritual journey, and God has placed them there for a purpose. God also places us in our respective departments to be a light to our colleagues.

- *"In fact, everyone who wants to live a godly life in Christ Jesus will be persecuted* (2 Tim. 3:12); *Yet at the same time many even among the professors believed in Christ. But because of the deans and department heads they would not confess their faith for fear they would be put out of the academy"* (John 12:42–43). Fear of man or the desire for the approval of man can sometimes blind us to the higher priority of pleasing God. We must diligently guard our motives, always seeking first the approval of our Lord and Savior, Jesus Christ. It is also good to remember that while we don't welcome the scorn of colleagues, the absence of *any* persecution as we walk through life is a telltale sign of whether we have in fact lived "a godly life in Christ Jesus." Just play it to the audience of *one*.

Practical Ways to Minister to Students and Colleagues

Before moving on to various distinctive aspects of being a Christian academic, I want to mention those things that we share in common with our non-Christian colleagues. Our testimony to our students and colleagues begins with doing the very best we can in teaching, research, and service. Our students will not care how much we know until they know how much we care. Small things that are not time consuming (to be discussed in what follows) can go a long way toward communicating our love and concern for them. We must also be committed to excellence in the research work that we do, not allowing our Christian faith and activities to become an excuse for not providing our employer good value for what we are paid. Being a good citizen in our departments by doing at least our fair share in service is also an important part of my testimony. We must ask God to make us highly effective and efficient in doing "first things first," as Stephen Covey says in 7 *Habits of Highly Effective People* and in guiding us to fruitful areas of research.[1] Since we have other obligations to our churches, and probably spend more time on average with our families than our non-Christian colleagues, we need to be highly productive in the time that we invest in the academy, since we may be either unwilling or unable to spend the inordinate amount of time that is often typical of professors.

Ministering to Students

In *Blink*, Malcolm Gladwell makes the point that first impressions are often lasting, and little things often make a big difference.[2] If this is so, then the first class period of each course that we teach is extremely important in many ways. One of the most important goals for my first class is to connect personally with the students. After sharing about the course objectives and reviewing the syllabus, I share with them things that are interesting for them to know about me using photos of my family, me playing tennis, snow skiing, and flying a Cessna 172 that I rent as a private pilot. I then share with them that the most important thing I want them to know about me is that I am a Christian, and by that, I don't just mean going to church, but rather that my Christian faith is the foundation on which everything else that I do is built. I then add that I hope that they will see that it makes a difference in how I treat them in this class. Finally, I tell the students that if they are interested in more details about how and why I became a Christian as a college student, they can read about my spiritual journey at www.LeaderU.com, under "faculty offices." By having this information available at the LeaderU.com web site, they will

---

1. Stephen Covey, 7 *Habits of Highly Effective People* (New York: Simon and Schuster, 1989).
2. Malcolm Gladwell, *Blink* (New York: Little, Brown, 2005).

also be exposed to many other Christian faculty and interesting articles on Christian apologetics.

To have a web site/faculty office at LeaderU.com, you need to register at www.facultylinc.com. You can then import your photo and other information into the template, making it very easy to set up your "faculty office," which will then be displayed at LeaderU.com.

At the end of the first class, I take the students' pictures in groups of four and bring printed copies to the second class and ask them to print their name on their picture. Using these pictures with names, I can usually learn each student's name by the end of the third week. This not only shows personal interest in them, but it facilitates classroom discussions when I can call on each student by name.

To continue to sow seeds with my students, my wife and I have a movie night one Friday night per month. We invite the students to come for pizza and for a movie that will both entertain and raise interesting questions about life. Movies we have used include *Crimes and Misdemeanors, Groundhog Day, Chariots of Fire, Citizen Kane, Out of Africa, Contact,* and *Quiz Show.* I typically have ten to fifteen students come, and we usually have a good thirty-minute discussion after the movie, centered on the important question(s) about life raised by the movie. These are wonderful times of getting to know the student personally and having an appropriate context to share with them how I view the world as a Christian. A detailed description of how a movie night might be done is available at www.facultylinc.com under "best practices."

At the end of the semester, I offer my students the gift of a book. This works particularly well in the fall as the semester finishes just before Christmas. I particularly like *The Case for Christ* by Lee Strobel.[3] I make these available to the students at the final exam in a box by the door so that they can pick up a copy if they choose. I tell them that Strobel was a famous reporter for the *Chicago Tribune* with a law degree from Yale who was challenged to explore the validity of the Christian truth claims by the changes that he saw in his wife when she became a Christian. He writes the book as an investigative reporter might, interviewing experts on ten critical questions and posing challenging questions to each expert. About half of my students will take a copy of the book. Some actually

3. Lee Strobel, *The Case for Christ* (Grand Rapids: Zondervan, 1998).

read it and become Christians; some already are Christians but are strengthened in their faith.

I also take opportunities where the subject matter permits to include a Christian point of view. Engineering ethics is a good example. Ethical systems may be based on philosophical arguments, humanistic values, or religious beliefs. It is appropriate to be comprehensive when addressing such topics by including a discussion of Christian ethics. Additionally, the universe is finely designed in so many ways, and this provides wonderful examples of God's fingerprints through his creation that I can point to from time to time in class. Finally, I take the opportunity to bring to students' attention special events on campus, including events sponsored by various Christian groups on campus (including our Christian Faculty Network).

In the fall of 1999 I did a simple experiment to see how the seeds that I had been planting over the years might be doing. I had one hundred students, evenly distributed between two classes, who produced 150 hits on my testimony at LeaderU.com from Texas A&M University within one week of my invitation to my classes to "check it out," suggesting that most did and some recommended it to friends. Our three movie nights drew about sixty students in total, although some were repeaters. About half took books at the end of the semester. At the final exam, I told the students that I would e-mail their grade on the final and their final course grade if they would put their e-mail address on their exam. (Before the days of Blackboard and WebCT, these were not so readily available.) When I sent out their grades, I also included an attachment with a personal note, reminding them of my comments at the beginning of the semester and inviting them to join me in a four-week seekers' Bible study on the gospel of John at the beginning of the spring semester. I was delighted to have thirteen students indicate an interest, and in January I had thirteen come to this study. We had a wonderful time together and several students became Christians, while the rest came to understand more clearly who Jesus claimed to be and what remarkable things he offers us. Paul was a student in my class that semester. Here is a note he sent to me the day after he got his PhD in Biomedical Engineering at Texas A&M University:

> You may use these photos wherever and whenever you like. I have shared my testimony with many over the last few years, and I always

point to the group discussion at your house (after watching *Crimes
and Misdemeanors*), the Bible study you led on campus covering the
book of John, and the letter you sent me while I was in the German
hospital as turning points in my belief. Those things that you did, I
hope to emulate when I am a professor, because I have seen first-hand
the impact a Christian professor can have on bringing his students to
a relationship with Jesus. You can quote me on that.

Amy read Strobel's book and came to Christ directly over the
summer. She came back in the fall so excited, wanting four additional
copies of the book to give to the various members of her family. Jason
is a National Merit Scholar whose spiritual interest was pricked
during the semester he was in my class. He came back to discuss
his interest in Jesus Christ two semesters after he took my class as
God continued to water the seeds that I had sown. As we studied
Strobel's book and the gospel of John, Jason came to faith in Christ
and was baptized.

In summary, by creating a web site at LeaderU.com, taking a
couple of evenings to have students over for a movie, offering a free
book, or reaching out to your students in other ways with which
you are comfortable, you can be a blessing and witness for Christ
to your students. In turn, you will be blessed by what God will do
in their lives and in your life as you take these steps to be faithful to
the opportunities God so abundantly provides in the academy.

Furthermore, imagine what might happen on your campus if
each Christian professor were willing to spend the small amount
of time described above sowing. At Texas A&M University, we had
2,500 professors, with at least 10 percent or 250 who were Christians.
If each professor teaches two hundred students per year, then fifty
thousand students each year would be impacted by a Christian
professor, or essentially the entire student body of forty-five thousand
students. Each student would likely have four such professors during
their four years at TAMU. If their results were similar to mine,
then they would collectively generate 6,500 (250 x 13 x 2) excellent
prospects for seeker Bible studies each year, enough to swamp all
of the student Christian groups on campus with students whom
God has touched and who are interested in learning more about the
possibilities of a personal relationship with Jesus Christ.

Ministering to colleagues may be divided into two areas: colleagues
who are already Christians and colleagues who are not but might

be open. What are some ways that I might reach out to all of my professional colleagues?

Ministering to Christian Colleagues

I previously mentioned that getting together regularly for sharing, prayer, mutual encouragement, or the study of the Bible or a relevant book is essential if Christian professors are going to not just survive, but thrive. Inviting a small group of friends from your area of the campus to get together for lunch can be a very rewarding experience, for them and for you.

A next step might be to find several Christian professors who would like to pursue a discipleship program designed especially for Christian faculty. Rae Mellichamp and Bill Hager have put together just such a program (see "Best Practices" at facultylinc.com). I took a group of five colleagues from across the campus at TAMU through this discipleship program, meeting every Monday morning for breakfast. These smiling faces at 6:15 a.m. at Denny's are testimony to the special grace that God gives when we are willing to follow his calling. It was an extremely rewarding experience for each of us, trying to live our lives with a set of priorities that more consistently reflected our Christian values (1 Thess. 5:24), growing in our relationship with Jesus Christ, and being equipped to sow broadly in our areas of influence on campus.

Many other excellent ideas for ministering to Christian colleagues may be found at facultylinc.com under "Best Practices," such as Rae Mellichamp's new book, Go Fast, Turn Left on living out of your priorities.[4]

Ministering to Non-Christian Colleagues

I think our ministry to our non-Christian colleagues begins with taking a genuine interest in them as people and avoiding the trap of seeing them as targets for evangelism. Taking advantage of opportunities to be helpful to them and to serve them builds bridges across which God's love can be taken. Being patient and waiting for God to open doors of opportunity is also essential.

---

4. Rae Mellichamp, Go Fast, Turn Left (Addison, TX: Lewis & Stanley, 2006).

Facultylinc.com has excellent resources on how to be a great teacher, how to make tenure, and how to manage your time, all topics that are of keen interest to new, tenure-track professors. Try them yourself and then share them with colleagues. While department head of Mechanical Engineering at Texas A&M University, I took the training to become a certified Franklin-Covey facilitator for *7 Habits of Highly Effective People,* one of the best programs available on getting into focus and staying there. I then offered this twenty-four-hour-long workshop each semester for about thirty to forty professors as a service to the university. It was extremely well received by Christian and non-Christian professors alike, from Mechanical Engineering, the College of Engineering, and from across the university. It was a wonderful way to provide a very valuable service to these professors and establish a friendship with them, which often led to opportunities to discuss spiritual things—especially when they where trying to prepare their mission statements.

When I was teaching in Colorado, we set aside one night per month to have various non-Christian couples over for dinner. This was a simple but effective way to get to know my non-Christian colleagues and for Ann to get to know their spouses. Ask God to help you see creative ways that you can serve your colleagues at your university.

Once you develop some meaningful relationships with your non-Christian colleagues, there are many creative ways to engage them in discussion of the bigger issues of life and their spiritual journey. *The Journey* by Peter Kreeft is a wonderful book for discussing whether truth can be known by exploring the "isms" of the twentieth century such as skepticism, cynicism, and relativism.[5] One year, I invited eight non-Christian friends to go on this "journey" with me in search of truth. Each read the first chapter in the book I gave them, and found it so intriguing that all but one came to the lunchtime discussion. This led very naturally into a study of the gospel of John. Three people from the group became Christians, and the others finished the study well on their way. Some of my very best friends, Christian and non-Christian, were formed from that experience.

A Discussion/Dessert series is also a great format for engaging non-Christian friends in discussions about God and life. Six couples

---

5. Peter Kreeft, *The Journey* (Downers Grove, IL: InterVarsity, 1996).

or singles cohost the four week series and invite five non-Christian singles or couples using invitations prepared by the group but distributed personally. This provides a group of twenty to thirty for the discussion, with more non-Christians than Christians. A fifty-nine minute discussion utilizing questions posed by the guests is followed by dessert and great discussion spring boarding off of the fifty-nine minute larger group discussion. There can be great sowing during the series and often some subsequent reaping. I had a colleague offer to buy my lunch at the faculty club to discuss two pressing questions that he had: why do you have to believe that Christ is God to be a Christian and how and why did I become a Christian. What a double treat, a free lunch and the opportunity to discuss these two very important questions. Many more ideas are available at facultylinc.com under "best practices," so check it out.

A Christian Perspective on Research and That Outrageous Idea

Why publish or perish? Research and the resulting scholarly publications have become a normal expectation at most universities today, with the demands growing rapidly at some universities. Let me share three perspectives professors might have as they view the opportunity and obligation to produce research results and publish them. The first view should be avoided while the second and third views should be happily embraced by Christian professors. First, the *cynical view* sees publishing as a meaningless game required in the academy to avoid perishing. Second, the *Christian stewardship view* sees the time (and sometime money) made available to academics for their scholarly pursuits as bringing an obligation to discover seminal insights in our respective fields and to make these ideas available to the public who ultimately pays, either directly or indirectly, for us to have the opportunity to engage in scholarship. Publishing in archival journals is one way to fulfill this obligation. Third, the *Christian love view* suggests that as we engage in research, God will give us significant insights that are to be shared with other people to make their lives better and their appreciation of God and his goodness greater. I am highly motivated if I think of my research and writing as an integral part of how I can serve God by serving his people and helping them to see God more clearly.

How to Find a Golden Research Topic

By far the most important step in being successful in research is the selection of a problem to be studied. I think the analogy of gold mining is most helpful. Mining a "tapped out" gold mine with great skill and diligence will not produce a significant amount of gold. Prospecting to find a mine rich in gold ore is critical to being a good steward of the time and resources we consume doing research. But prospecting takes time, patience, and skill. The path of least resistance in the short run is to just keep mining where you have been, whether or not it is still a productive mine.

Let me share a few suggestions on prospecting for a good claim where the mine you find is rich in gold. First, pray! It is amazing how we often forget the obvious. God sees my field, my talents and abilities, my best opportunities. Who better to guide and direct me to fruitful areas where I might invest my research time? I encourage my Christian graduate students to pray daily about their selection of a PhD topic and then about the journey of discovery that they will be taking, that God will guide and direct their steps along the way and lead them to significant discoveries.

Second, search out every nook and cranny of your field for emerging ideas and trends. Being early to engage in a developing area means you get to harvest the low hanging fruit; coming later means you get to harvest the high hanging fruit, which is much more time-consuming. Read broadly, brainstorm with colleagues, visit potential collaborators or sponsors, and learn to be a good listener. Too often we are too eager to talk and not sufficiently interested in listening during such meetings. However, we learn little or nothing when we are talking. I think it is no accident that God gave us two ears and one mouth; it is at least twice as hard to listen as it is to talk (and also to make our hearing more bi-directional).

Attending national meetings is a way to also spot trends. Don't just camp out in sessions that are focused on what you already do. Take time to visit a variety of venues and especially the plenary sessions, where the speakers are often selected because of new groundbreaking work that they are doing. I also have found that attending smaller meetings formatted to allow longer, invited presentations of cutting-edge work in progress with significant time for discussion following the presentations to be the best way to identify significant, emerging areas. Gordon Research Conferences held at small colleges in the summer or early January are the best example in my field. The conferences include three informal meals each day with colleagues from across the country, allowing stimulating discussions of new ideas that often surpass the formal presentations in value. Finally, read widely outside of the technical literature in your field. Some of your most brilliant ideas will come from the most unexpected places. In 1977, I read in the *Wall Street Journal* (not technical literature for materials scientists) that Ford Motors hoped to make its automobiles almost entirely out of plastics and composites by the year 2000. It was this article that caused me to make a major career move toward engineering plastics and composites, ramping down my work in metals and alloys. I was fortunate to be early into this emerging field and became established as a major player, which meant I was able to get an abundance of research funding for the next twenty years with a minimum of effort.

During my tenure as department head of Mechanical Engineering at Texas A&M University, I had the occasion to do annual reviews for sixty-seven professors. Success was not simply correlated with either raw intelligence or diligence. The choice of a fruitful research area and the willingness to change as that area became mature were the dominant factors. Don't let fear of change or laziness keep you mining a secure but empty gold mine. Become a prospector.

Extending Your Reach with the Outrageous Idea of Christian Scholarship

The previous discussions of ministry in this chapter focused on approaches that will have an immediate impact on your campus. However, scholarship has the potential to reach a much larger audience and greatly increase the impact that you can make for the kingdom. George Marsden's book, *The Outrageous Idea of Christian Scholarship*,[6] is excellent background reading as you consider how your scholarship might be used of God to make "not just an impression but an impact," to quote my good friend, Dr. Rick Rigsby.

What is scholarship? It is the pursuit of *truth*. There are at least two ways that our Christian worldview should impact our scholarship. The first way is well stated by C. S. Lewis: "I believe in Christianity as

6. George Marsden, *The Outrageous Idea of Christian Scholarship* (Oxford: Oxford University Press, 1997).

I believe that the Sun has risen, not only because I see it, but because by it I see everything else."[7] Christianity provides a different kind of light that will give us insights that we will not find by just "poking" around, much like black light (ultraviolet wavelengths) will cause a display that is sensitive to ultraviolet light to radiate, allowing one to see things that simply are not visible within the normal visible spectrum of radiation. A second way that our Christian worldview should impact our scholarship is in the questions that we find most interesting. For example:

- Dave Larson's studies of the relationship of religious beliefs to physical and emotional health;
- Byron Johnson's studies of the effect of Christian conversion with Bible study on prison recidivism;
- David G. Myers's studies of what makes a person happy;
- Ev Worthington's study of forgiveness;
- Jan Swearingen's study of how pulpit oratory shaped the language of the Declaration of Independence;
- Ralph Wood's study of the literature works of Flannery O'Connor and J. R. R. Tolkien;
- Bradford Wilcox's study of the institution of marriage.

On a more personal level, one might ask how this applies in engineering; for example, how does a Christian bridge differ from the usual bridge that one might build? My answer is found in a bridge that our engineering students and professors helped Harmon Parker, the founder and director of Bridging the Gap Africa, build in Kenya. The design of this pedestrian bridge is not unique, but our interest in designing and building it in a very remote location in Kenya was motivated by our Christian concern to help people on the far side of the river. This bridge will save approximately two million miles of walking per year at a price of $5,000.

We are designing a 420-foot pedestrian bridge to cross the second largest river in Kenya. We have found a few examples of pedestrian bridges this long, but they cost more than $500,000, use composite materials that are not available in Kenya, and would require construction equipment that cannot reach the remote location

---

7. C. S. Lewis, "Is Theology Poetry," in *The Weight of Glory* (San Francisco: Harper Collins, 1980 ed.), 140.

where this bridge is desperately needed. My students' challenge is to design a bridge that can be built for $100,000 using materials that are readily available in Kenya, without the assistance of large construction equipment. This is a much more challenging design project than designing such a bridge for construction in the United States with a budget of $500,000.

My work on designing and building bridges is one aspect of a larger research initiative that I have started at Baylor on appropriate technology for developing countries. I have sensed God leading me to focus my engineering research to serve the poorest two billion people in the world who live on less than two dollars per day. Rather than helping to make the most comfortable billion people a little more comfortable, God wants me to help the poorest of the poor have a better shot at survival, with their most basic human needs being met.

I began this initiative collaborating with my former student and dear Christian brother, Dr. John Pumwa, the first person from Papua New Guinea to earn a PhD in engineering and currently the department head of Mechanical Engineering at UniTech, the only engineering school in Papua New Guinea. Coconuts are an abundant, renewable resource that grows within 20° of the equator. Within this band, only Singapore is a fully developed country. Our goal is to use coconuts to provide electricity, building materials, fuel for cooking, and other value-added products using technology that is suitable for rural villages. Electricity will in turn make possible the storage of medicines, the use of old computers in schools, clean lighting in the evening, and the inexpensive production of sodium hypochlorite for water purification. It will also open new doors of opportunity for other kinds of economic development, creating jobs and economic opportunity, which are desperately needed in the developing world. But how is this possible?

Through our research we have learned that coconut oil has the best chemical properties of the more than fifty vegetable oils that have been studied for making bio-diesel. We have made coconut bio-diesel, and it burns beautifully in standard diesel engines. We have also demonstrated that pure coconut oil preheated to 90°C can be burned in a diesel engine directly without first converting it to coconut bio-diesel. We have found that we can make binderless particle board from the husk by just hot pressing at a suitable temperature and pressure. The coconut shell can be finely ground and used as reinforcement in engineering plastics or it can be used for simultaneously cooking and making charcoal. With an initial investment of six cents, we can convert coconuts into products worth sixty cents. We will be doing our first proof-of-concept project in Papua New Guinea in 2007 to demonstrate how the quality of life and economic opportunities can be dramatically improved in rural villages where coconuts grow, simply by using appropriate technology.

If this proof-of-concept project, which is receiving financial support from the United Nations, is successful, then my research group at Baylor can help rural villages around the world where coconuts are abundant to get World Bank loans and start similar enterprises. We will work with Christians in these villages to be sure that the economic opportunities and benefits are as fairly distributed as possible and that the project is part of a larger kingdom-building activity.

Especially exciting is the invitation I recently received to attend a planning workshop sponsored by the National Science Foundation, which is interested in research that would foster sustainable, global development. If the NSF begins to fund activities in this area, it will provide more resources. It will also make it a more academically respectable area in which to conduct research, which is not my concern as a tenured, distinguished professor who is sixty-three years old, but is certainly of concern to my younger colleagues.

One final personal example of how my faith has impacted my research has to do with my studies of the origin of life. As a scientist who is a Christian, I have always been interested in issues at the interface between faith and science, including such topics as whether scientific discoveries strengthen or undermine belief in God and how one might properly interpret the first eleven chapters of Genesis. God could obviously have worked in his customary way (as described by the laws or patterns in nature) or in some extraordinary way (usually described as miracles). But it is the question of how God brought life into being that has always been a particularly fascinating question for me. My professional work in polymer science and engineering (I served as the director of the Polymer Technology Center at Texas A&M University for ten years) provided me with the necessary tools to do original work in the origin of life. My research insights in this area have been published in *The Mystery of Life's Origin: Reassessing Current Theories,*[8] "A Statistical Examination of Self-Ordering of Amino Acids in Proteins,"[9] "Origin of Life and Evolution in Biology Textbooks—A Critique,"[10] "Entropy, Information, and the Origin of Life,"[11] "Is There Scientific Evidence for the Existence of God?"[12] and "Information and the Origin of Life."[13] Several of these have been posted at my web site at LeaderU.com, where they get a total of 50,000 hits per year. What a wonderful way to extend my reach!

Conclusion

As I reflect over my past thirty-nine-year journey in the Academy, I am amazed at how God has so exceeded even my wildest expectations of what he might be able to do through my life. I was diagnosed with chronic lymphomatic leukemia (CLL) in 2006, and so my future is uncertain. This makes me all the more thankful that I did not wait until late in my career to give God his rightful place in my professional life and my personal life. I took my first university position to be a Christian professor, not just a professor who happened to be a Christian, and I am still learning each year more of what that implies. I look forward to reaching heaven where I will have my final "Post-tenure Review" and where I will learn the full impact that I had in the lives of my students and colleagues. I can hardly wait!

8. Walter Bradley, Charles Thaxton, and Roger Olsen, *The Mystery of Life's Origin: Reassessing Current Theories* (Dallas: Lewis & Stanley, 1984).

9. Walter Bradley, Randall Kok, and John Talyor, "A Statistical Examination of Self-Ordering of Amino Acids in Proteins," *Origin of Life and Evolution of the Biosphere* 18 (1988): 135–42.

10. Walter Bradley, Gordon Mills, and Malcolm Lancester, "Origin of Life and Evolution in Biology Textbooks: A Critique," *American Biology Teacher* 55 (1993): 78–83.

11. Walter Bradley, "Entropy, Information, and the Origin of Life," in *Debating Design*, ed. William Dembski and Michael Ruse (Cambridge: Cambridge University Press, 2004).

12. Walter Bradley, "Is There Scientific Evidence for the Existence of God?" in *Science: Christian Perspectives for the New Millennium*, ed. Stan Wallace, Paul Copan, and Scott Luley (Addison, TX: CLM & RZIM, 2003).

13. Walter L. Bradley and Charles B. Thaxton, "Information and the Origin of Life" in *The Creation Hypothesis*, ed. J. P. Moreland (Downers Grove, IL: Intervarsity Press, 1994).

Acknowledgment

I want to take this opportunity to acknowledge my partner and the love of my life in this journey through the academy. There is nothing that I have accomplished that has not been made possible, either directly or indirectly, through my wonderful travel partner for life, Carol Ann Bradley. She has been as involved as I have been, leading student Bible studies, opening our home to a whole host of events from Friday night movies to Discussion/Dessert series, even living in a dorm as a dorm grandparent for one year. Her love for Jesus and for people has been a constant source of inspiration and encouragement to me and many others and a key ingredient in what God has done through our ministry together. She is God's greatest gift to me after Jesus.

Discussion Questions

1. What are some other biblical principles you have found helpful as a Christian professor?
2. Share some other ways you have ministered to students.
3. How can something like a "faculty office" at LeaderU.com be a helpful tool in ministry?
4. Discuss ways you can identify yourself to students as a Christian on the first day of class.
5. Was there a Christian professor who made a profound impact in your life as a student?
6. What are some other ways you can minister to your colleagues?
   a. Christian?
   b. Non-Christian?
7. What was helpful in Dr. Bradley's discussion regarding finding a research topic?
8. What are some possible ways that God could use your specific discipline and the scholarship generated from within for kingdom building?

6

SPHERICAL COWS AND MARS HILL: A HEURISTIC APPROACH TO THE TWO TASKS

ROBERT KAITA

There is an old joke that goes like this.[1] Milk production at a dairy farm was low, so the farmer wrote to a local university, asking for help from academia. A multidisciplinary team of professors was assembled, headed by a theoretical physicist, and two weeks of intensive on-site investigation took place. The scholars then returned to the university, notebooks crammed with data, where the task of writing the report was left to the team leader. Shortly thereafter, the farmer received the write-up, and opened it to read the first line: "Consider a spherical cow. . . ."

Apologies are offered to those who do not immediately find this amusing. To understand the joke, you have to realize that the physical sciences have been very successful in explaining a wide variety of natural phenomena. Since they are based on mathematics, however,

---

1. Recounted by John Harte in his book, *Consider a Spherical Cow: A Course in Environmental Problem Solving* (Sausalito, CA: University Science Books, 1988).

you have to first make simplifying assumptions to be able to do the calculations. For example, common sense would dictate that a complete description of the earth must include everything from the majesty of the Grand Canyon to the soaring peaks of the Himalayas. To physicists, in contrast, the earth is just a rather dull point mass if you want to calculate its orbit around the sun.

There is admittedly nothing that takes the fun out of a joke more than having to explain it. The truth reflected in the one above about academic research remains, nevertheless, because it carries to the absurd extreme a principle that is quite valuable in our work. It is based on what we call *heuristic* models. A dictionary defines a "heuristic" as something that serves to "guide, discover, or reveal."[2] The definition further elaborates with the remark that a heuristic is specifically "valuable for empirical research but unproved or incapable of proof."[3] It takes little more than a look outside your window to "prove" that the earth is not a point mass, and few would ask for "proof" that real cows are not spherical. As inaccurate as these descriptions might be, the simplifications they introduce, nonetheless, can show us how to approach the problems we really want to solve.

What does this have to do with *The Two Tasks of the Christian Scholar*? Recall Malik's description of the two tasks. The first task is based on the fact that "materially, politically, and morally, the Protestants of America command absolutely unprecedented resources, and spiritually they are in a state of creative ferment."[4] He claims that "Protestantism emphasizes four fundamental truths: the supreme importance of the Bible, both Old and New Testaments, as the Word of God; Jesus Christ of Nazareth as the Living Lord of lords and King of kings, with whom we must, and indeed we can, have a direct personal relationship; justification by faith and not by works, which is best expressed by Romans 4:5 (KJV), 'But to him that worketh not, but believeth on him that justifieth the ungodly, his faith is counted for righteousness'; and individual, personal, responsible freedom as the very essence of the dignity of man."[5]

2. *Webster's Seventh New College Dictionary*, (Springfield, MA: G. and C. Merriam Company, 1972).

3. Ibid.

4. See page 56 in chapter 2.

5. See pages 56–57 in chapter 2.

The first task is for Protestants to fulfill their "appointed destiny" as bearers of these truths. Malik calls us to evangelize, and to be effective in this, he cites three requirements: "greater unity among themselves (some of whom are hardly on speaking terms with others); greater understanding and mutual toleration between the evangelicals among them (although all Christians, by definition, are evangelical) and the more established churches; and rediscovering and appropriating the infinite riches of the great traditions: Orthodox, Catholic, and Protestant."[6]

Malik then goes on to say that "if evangelization is the most important task, the task that comes immediately after it—not in the tenth place, nor even the third place, but in the second place—is not politics, nor economics, nor the quest for comfort and security and ease, but to find out exactly what is happening to the mind and spirit in the schools and universities."[7] His primary purpose is to raise the issue of the "crisis" in academia, as far as Christianity's role in it is concerned, as the second of the two tasks. Although Malik speaks wistfully of a Christian university that has Ivy League stature, he readily admits that he has no easy formula for how that might be achieved. Rather than dealing with all facets of this seemingly unsolvable problem, however, there is merit in considering how certain aspects of it may still be addressed. While heuristic simplifications might seem naïve, they can help us get started.

The Heuristic Approach in Evangelism

We have an excellent example of how effective the heuristic approach can be in the book of Acts. There, we find that Paul uses this technique when he addresses his Athenian audience. His goal is clearly to evangelize, which is the first of the two tasks. However, Paul does not neglect the mind in two very important aspects. To begin with, he thinks about his listeners and tries to understand them. Instead of using theological jargon, for example, he is able to communicate effectively by respecting their worship of an "Unknown God." Paul then skillfully crafts his argument, utilizing poets and writers familiar to his audience. In that way, he enables his listeners

---

6. See page 57 in chapter 2.
7. See page 59 in chapter 2.

to understand who this God truly is, and recognize their need to repent before him.

To see how this comes about, let us begin by looking at Acts 17:16–34. The basic story is very well-known, but let us read the passage from the perspective of those who are familiar with academia today. We may be surprised to find those of us in the twenty-first century have much more in common with our predecessors in the first century than we might suspect.

The setting is Athens, where Paul is waiting for his fellow travelers Silas and Timothy. Beginning in verses 16–17, we read the following:

> While Paul was waiting for them in Athens, he was greatly distressed to see that the city was full of idols. So he reasoned in the synagogue with the Jews and the God-fearing Greeks, as well as in the marketplace day by day with those who happened to be there.

In a general sense, Christians today face the same challenges as Paul did from the "idols" worshiped by society at large. It is impressive how many of their images flash by during commercial television breaks, and their appearance on web sites has shown how technology ensures that they are inescapable. Paul confronted the problem wherever he could, whether in places of worship or in the marketplace. As members of the broader Christian community, we are called to do the same, whether it is to encourage fellow believers in church or to share the gospel where we live and work.

There is, however, another aspect of Paul's witness that has to do specifically with where he was located. Although politically and economically, Greece had been eclipsed by Rome at the time of Paul, Athens continued to be emblematic of its "Golden Age." The philosophical ideas from that era helped shape the Roman world, and indeed, influence us to this day. This makes it understandable why Paul is particularly disturbed by the presence of idols in that city. It still had a vibrant intellectual community, and for many, a literal belief in a multiplicity of gods was not an issue. However, Paul recognized that it was just as dubious, if not dangerous, to pursue ideas whose primary worth was their novelty.

Paul's concern thus has particular relevance to modern academia, where unfortunately, the latest fashion can take precedence over time-honored content. We see how he addresses the issue on his own "campus" as we read further in the chapter (Acts 17:18–21):

> A group of Epicurean and Stoic philosophers began to dispute with him. Some of them asked, "What is this babbler trying to say?" Others remarked, "He seems to be advocating foreign gods." They said this because Paul was preaching the good news about Jesus and the resurrection. Then they took him and brought him to a meeting of the Areopagus, where they said to him, "May we know what this new teaching is that you are presenting? You are bringing some strange ideas to our ears, and we want to know what they mean." (All the Athenians and the foreigners who lived there spent their time doing nothing but talking about and listening to the latest ideas.)

I taught a Sunday school lesson on this passage to a class of undergraduate and graduate students from local colleges. There were quite a few smirks of acknowledgment when we got to the last sentence. The serious point here is that we should take advantage of the natural tendencies of those with whom we associate. While being called a "babbler" is not flattering, you get the sense that Paul was not singled out for this title because he was a Christian. To this day, you often hear people muttering that they did not know what the speaker was "babbling about" as you leave a seminar. This does not prevent them from returning for more, however, and so it was for the apostle Paul.

Just a few chapters earlier, we read in Acts 14:19 that those who disagreed with him "stoned Paul and dragged him outside the city, thinking he was dead." This time, Paul's new colleagues, whom he met at the "Athenian Conference of Epicureans and Stoics," as it were, invited him to give a colloquium on his "new teaching" in the Department of Philosophy at "Aeropagus U."

The apostle Paul accepts the invitation. He is an excellent speaker who knows his audience well. As such, it is worthwhile to read his presentation in its entirety (Acts 17:22–31):

> Paul then stood up in the meeting of the Areopagus and said, "Men of Athens! I see that in every way you are very religious. For as I walked around and looked carefully at your objects of worship, I even found an altar with this inscription: TO AN UNKNOWN GOD. Now what you worship as something unknown I am going to proclaim to you.

"The God who made the world and everything in it is the Lord of heaven and earth and does not live in temples built by hands. And he is not served by human hands, as if he needed anything, because he himself gives all men life and breath and everything else. From one man he made every nation of men, that they should inhabit the whole earth; and he determined the times set for them and the exact places where they should live. God did this so that men would seek him and perhaps reach out for him and find him, though he is not far from each one of us. For in him we live and move and have our being. As some of your own poets have said, 'We are his offspring.'

"Therefore since we are God's offspring, we should not think that the divine being is like gold or silver or stone—an image made by man's design and skill. In the past God overlooked such ignorance, but now he commands all people everywhere to repent. For he has set a day when he will judge the world with justice by the man he has appointed. He has given proof of this to all men by raising him from the dead."

The apostle Paul crafts his remarks to be consonant with a worldview familiar to his audience. As a good speaker, he piques the interest of his listeners with the irony of bringing their "Unknown God" to the fore. Paul asserts that this God is the one who created everything, including his listeners. This God distinguishes himself from all other gods in that he does not require us to serve him. Rather, all God has done causes us to seek him.

Therefore, Paul brilliantly argues, if his hearers are looking for the true God, the God Paul proclaims is the one whom they seek. Once you know who this God is, furthermore, you have no excuse for disobeying him. God demands that we repent, lest the Judge he appointed judges us. We know who this Judge is, Paul concludes, since God raised this Judge from the dead.

This is all well and good, but it is also informative to realize what Paul did not say. He mentions God "who made the world and everything in it," but does not uniquely associate him with the God of Abraham, Isaac, and Jacob. Instead, he seems to allow that this God is part of the Greek pantheon, albeit not the least of its members as some may have thought. Furthermore, Paul speaks of our need for repentance, and tells us of the resurrected one who will judge us. However, he does not call Jesus Christ by name, nor does he explain how Christ's death has covered the sins for which we should be repentant. To be fair, Paul is forthright about mentioning Christ earlier in the chapter, but not during his colloquium at Aeropagus U.

Was Paul, the greatest of Christian evangelists, a compromiser? Was he delinquent in failing to preach the gospel accurately? Not at all. From the time he spent in the marketplace each day, Paul became very familiar with how his audience thought. He was aware that he had a hard case to make, and he knew he would not be able to do it all at once. We have evidence for this at the end of the chapter, where we read the following (Acts 17:32–34):

> When they heard about the resurrection of the dead, some of them sneered, but others said, "We want to hear you again on this subject." At that, Paul left the Council. A few men became followers of Paul and believed. Among them was Dionysius, a member of the Areopagus, also a woman named Damaris, and a number of others.

Paul recognized that if the audience did not accept the resurrection of the dead, he could never get to the atoning work of Christ. By his own later words in 1 Corinthians 15:17, "if Christ has not been raised, your faith is futile; you are still in your sins." Some were contemptuous of the thought, but others wanted to learn more. Paul's heuristic approach, while seemingly inaccurate at first glance, was thus vindicated. Note also that the passage tells of only a few becoming followers of Paul, lest we think that numbers are the only measure of our effectiveness.

What are the practical implications of this message? For the first of the two tasks, we see how we might achieve the unity Malik calls for among Christians. Serious doctrinal differences, of course, should not be taken lightly. However, the focus of both Malik and Paul is in evangelization. We might still be tempted, perhaps, to criticize those who evangelize with others who have differing views on the sacraments. This, however, would be just as misguided as castigating Paul for failing to mention Jesus Christ by name on Mars Hill. There are Christians of all traditions who share the four truths mentioned at the outset of this chapter, and have a burning desire to tell them to the world. They should be seen not as enemies, but as co-workers in the Great Commission.

The key point is that we must know our audience, as Paul did. To demonstrate how important this is, let me describe two different venues for presentations that I gave near my home institution. The first was at a college close to Princeton. The evening began with the presentation of an excellent video, based on the book *The Privileged Planet* by Guillermo Gonzalez and Jay W. Richards.[8] Gonzalez is an astronomer at the Iowa State University, and Richards is a philosopher at the Discovery Institute in Seattle, Washington.

The basic thesis of both the book and the video is that if you consider all that is needed for life to exist, the probability of finding a place that satisfies them is very small. Scientists used to think that there were relatively few requirements for a planet to support life, like being a solid body similar to the earth and having the right distance from some convenient star. Given the number of stars in our galaxy, this should mean that there were plenty of places where life could exist. Such an assumption was the stock-in-trade of popular television shows like *Star Trek*. As you followed the voyages of the starship "Enterprise" across our galaxy, we were not supposed to be surprised that there were so many planets with beautiful women who were charmed by its heroic captain, James T. Kirk.

Recent research, however, has shown that the list of requirements for life is not so short. Stars with planets having life on them have to be about the same mass and brightness as our sun. Bigger ones, for example, burn themselves out too quickly. We also cannot be too close to the center of our galaxy. Otherwise, there would be too much radiation there for life to be comfortable. Perhaps the most unexpected and remarkable requirement for life is the existence of our moon. It is so big compared to the earth that it has a stabilizing effect on its motion, and hence its climate. As an added bonus, it has just the right size and orbit so that intelligent observers on earth can learn about the sun during solar eclipses.

This list has not been compiled by fanatics with religious agendas, but by sober, mainstream scientists. It goes on and on, so that the probability of finding a planet that satisfies all of the requirements for life gets to be quite small. The earth is thus a very "privileged" planet, and it also appears to have special properties that help intelligent beings find out about the nature of the universe.

The video presented this case with clarity and excellent "production values," and the showing was followed by a time where I addressed

8. Guillermo Gonzales and Jay W. Richards, *The Privileged Planet: How Our Place in the Cosmos Is Designed for Discovery* (Washington, DC: Regnery Publishing, 2004).

questions from the audience. There was a standing-room-only crowd of more than 140 people who were mostly students and faculty from the college. The technical questions about physics and astronomy were quite straightforward for me to answer. I just had to elaborate on the points I mentioned above, and given the chance, I would have gladly waxed poetical about fascinating concepts like black holes in the center of our galaxy. However, most of the questions had to do with "intelligent design," or ID. They were primarily rhetorical, like "Isn't ID an attempt by right-wing religious fundamentalists to get their faith into the classroom?" or "If the debate is really about science, why is tonight's event just sponsored by Christian groups?" I answered them by sticking to the scientific methodology that was the basis for the video. It was telling that after I explained this several times, subsequent questioners said they understood this. However, they still wanted their "questions" answered in their own way, and several were getting quite testy.

As frustrating as it was, this did not bother me, as I felt that they were simply looking for affirmation of their preconceived notions, rather than trying to learn anything new. I consoled myself with the possibility that if a scientist like me did not affirm them, they might be challenged to change their thinking in the future. What I did find trying was the fact that the very repetitive questioning went on for a full three hours. The "evolution," as it were, from an evening that I thought was going to focus on thought-provoking findings in physics and astronomy into a "battle" over ID was not surprising, considering how much it has been in the news. It was disappointing, on the other hand, because my expertise as a scientist was clearly of little relevance.

On several occasions, I was very tempted to say that if I were not a Christian, I would not be standing in front of them. Was the evening then a failure because I did not explicitly mention Christ? I do not think so. If I did make such an admission, it would have probably stopped the dialogue then and there. While sparing my voice, it would have been at the cost of affirming the preconceptions of a "religious agenda" that the most confrontational of the students had. By thus marginalizing me, the need to grapple with the evidence for a Creator so wonderfully articulated in *The Privileged Planet* would be lost.

I later found out that the Christians in the audience appreciated this. They were kind enough to tell me afterward that the way I handled loaded questions from the audience and avoided the "fight" that many expected but never materialized, was a witness that encouraged them. As a specific exciting development, I learned long after the meeting that there was an undergraduate physics student who began his spiritual journey that evening. He subsequently had Bible studies with several students, and he ultimately accepted Jesus Christ as his Lord and Savior. Such news should encourage us to be as generous as we can with our sowing, even if the soil does not look too promising at first.

A short while later, I was asked by an old friend of mine, a chaplain at my home institution to participate in a panel discussion. The dormitories there are divided into so-called residential colleges, each with its own dining hall and advisors called "fellows," who have responsibilities including organizing special events for the students. The chaplain is one such person, and he invited me to join one of his college's dinner and discussion programs. A professor of philosophy who was also a Christian joined me, and the topic for the evening was entitled the "Harmony of Science and Belief in God." After introducing ourselves and giving brief testimonies to our faith, the floor was open to questions from the audience.

Like the event at the local college, the venue was also secular. It was clear from the start, however, that the atmosphere was far less confrontational. Several of the students were quite outspoken about their Christian beliefs, and the skeptics were polite in their questioning. During the course of the evening, the philosophy professor made some excellent points. He said he tells his students that they should not believe in anything that does not have a rational basis. He also pointed out that you had a lot more explaining to do if you claimed you were the Son of God than if you held that Jesus Christ was the Son of God.

These were perfect segues for introducing the rational basis for our belief in God and in Jesus Christ specifically as his only Son. I was able to speak comfortably about Christ's resurrection as a singular historical event, as well as his death for our sins that preceded it. The need to argue for the existence of God never came up during the evening. In this context, to fail to progress beyond what was not at issue would have been a less than effective witness.

Note that in both instances, I did not actively seek the opportunity to speak. I freely confess that as a physicist at a major research institution, my first inclination is to think that I am much too busy for this. On the other hand, I am aware that Christ must be known as much in the twenty-first century as he was in the first. This is what motivates me as scientist and a Christian to take on the first of the two tasks, that of witnessing to the redemption we have through Jesus Christ.

The Heuristic Approach and the Mind and Spirit in Science

For both of the two tasks, there is no denying that the mind has to be engaged, first to appreciate those whom you are addressing and then to craft arguments that are appropriate for them. This is what Paul did, and we should clearly do likewise. Our responsibility as thinking Christians, however, does not end with an understanding of humanity's timeless need for salvation through Christ. As Malik puts it bluntly, he has "no patience with piety alone."[9]

Such a mindset may arguably be more of a problem in the sciences than the humanities. The conflict of worldviews is widely appreciated in the latter, and Malik goes to great lengths in describing its consequences in his *Two Tasks*. However, he has nothing but praise for the sciences. Taken at face value, then, it apparently does not matter what you believe as scientist, as long as you have mastered its methodology. Christians in the sciences are thus absolved of any concern about the second of the two tasks, as long as they are good scientists.

There are difficulties with this position, as explained elsewhere in this book.[10] Many, however, do not feel they have to address them to argue that a belief in God is relevant to the pursuit of science. They can simply attest, for example, to the way God has answered prayer with a solution to a thorny problem. While the capacity for God to do this is undeniable, however, this is not necessarily a persuasive argument for his existence for our unbelieving colleagues. Examples abound of how solutions suddenly appear after you "take your mind off" the original challenge. The phenomenon has been

9. See page 60 in chapter 2.
10. See chapter 4.

known since antiquity, and could be related to how our brains process information. Archimedes' discovery, while bathing, of how different elements displace unequal amounts of water is part of the folklore of science.

While a long, hot bath is a luxury few of us moderns can indulge in regularly, "eureka" moments still do often occur to scientists while taking a shower. The great physicist Richard Feynman apparently had similar experiences when he frequented clubs featuring "exotic dancers." His delightful informal autobiography, *Surely You're Joking, Mr. Feynman*, includes the following description of how he worked there. According to Feynman, he would "watch the girls dance, do a little physics, prepare a lecture, or draw a little bit. If I got a little tired, I'd watch the entertainment for awhile, and then do a little more work."[11]

Obviously, my intention is not to equate "adult entertainment" with prayer in any strict sense. Rather, I use this extreme example to suggest that in the particular case of perceived divine intervention, it could be attributed to nothing more than a quirk of human brain physiology. Just as unbelievers can be pious, they can be "inspired" as well. Who would criticize prayer if it works for you, our colleagues might say, but it is functionally no different from the "distractions" that worked for one of the greatest physicists of the twentieth century.

Can scientists, then, ask if there could be evidence for God that can be uncovered from their work? Many Christians are reluctant to do so, since they fear being labeled as believers in a "God of the gaps." A typical argument against such a belief in the supernatural is as follows: In times past, many people thought that angels moved the planets along their orbits. Now, we know that gravity is responsible, so the realm of influence for such beings is diminished. Eventually, their need disappears altogether, and so would our belief in them. We should thus be wary of anything that suggests a "designer" behind natural phenomena, so the argument goes, since science will eventually come up with a "natural" explanation for them.

The position so described is actually one of faith, and it commonly goes by the name "naturalism." Its tenet is that the supernatural does not exist, so scientific evidence for it is simply not possible.

11. Richard P. Feynman, *Surely You're Joking, Mr. Feynman! Adventures of a Curious Character* (New York: W. W. Norton, 1985).

Christians who unconditionally seek to avoid the "God of the gaps" criticism are thus ultimately taking on the belief system of those who deny the reality of God, and this is a tremendous cost to pay. Writers like Stephen Jay Gould, for example, offer what at first seems like an attractive way to avoid this dilemma. He speaks of so-called "non-overlapping magisteria," which has become commonly known by its acronym, NOMA.[12] In this picture, science holds sway in the physical world, while religion is master over the spiritual realm, and never the twain shall meet. The problem, however, is that it too easily allows us to equate the former with the objectively real, and the latter with subjective fantasy. It is like the imaginary axis in mathematics, which is so named because of its orthogonality to the "real" one.

For the position Christians should adopt instead, we can return to the approach taken by Paul. On the Aeropagus, he does not argue in some vague way about the value of believing in God, regardless of whether or not he "really" exists. Instead, Paul speaks about a God who is not a philosophical abstraction, but the one who will subject humanity to a very real final judgment. Under these circumstances, the repentance God demands is not the same as a vague intellectual assent to his reality, but a genuine change of heart. Even Gould might have belied a sense that the stakes are high in the dedication of his magnum opus, "The Structure of Evolutionary Theory." It reads as follows:

> For Niles Eldridge and Elisabeth Vrba
> May we always be the Three Musketeers
> Prevailing with panache
> From our manic and scrappy inception at Dijon
> To our nonsatanic and happy reception at Doomsday
> *All for one and one for all*[13]

Gould may have simply wanted to be poetic, but he does describe the final "reunion" with his colleagues in a very curious way.

The strong linkage with reality that Paul makes suggests that Christians as scientists must not do everything they can to avoid the

---

12. Stephen J. Gould, "Nonoverlapping Magisteria," *Natural History* 106 (1997): 16.

13. Dedication to Stephen Jay Gould, *The Structure of Evolutionary Theory* (Cambridge, MA: Harvard University Press, 2002).

"God of the gaps" criticism, but confront it in a very fundamental way. I am not talking about the cavalier attribution of anything that we presently do not understand to divine action. Rather, we should use science to discover all that we can about the physical world, but then not question the results of our research if they challenge our *a priori* metaphysical assumptions.

This can cut both ways. On the one hand, the discovery of the law of gravity may bring into the question the medieval belief that angels were necessary for planetary motion. On the other hand, we have the more modern example of Einstein and his general theory of relativity. In it, he introduced something called the "cosmologic constant" to his equations of gravitation. This was to avoid the so-called "time variability of the metric distance of two mass points," or in other words, to ensure a "steady state" universe.

Einstein's motivation was philosophical, not technical. Its consequence was that he missed out in making one of the greatest scientific predictions of all time. If Einstein had just stuck to the scientific implications of his equations, he could have foreseen Edwin Hubble's discovery that the universe was indeed expanding. He put it this way in the last edition of his book on relativity.

> If Hubble's expansion had been discovered at the time of the creation of the general theory of relativity, the cosmologic member [or constant] would never have been introduced. It seems now so much less justified to introduce such a member into the field equations, since its introduction loses its sole original justification,—that leading to a natural solution of the cosmologic problem.[14]

There is thus no guarantee that the conclusions we draw are scientifically correct when philosophical prejudice of any stripe comes into play.

As Christians who are scientists, then, we are expected to do the research to the best of our ability. We are to be as objective as we can in following where it leads us, and not assume, like Gould, that issues of faith fall outside of the "magisterium" of science. Consider, for example, the emphasis Paul puts on the resurrection of Jesus Christ. Can we envision a scenario by which its reality can be challenged scientifically? Time travel is impossible, but the next

---

14. Albert Einstein, *The Meaning of Relativity* (Princeton, NJ: Princeton University Press, 1956).

best thing is the historical record. Imagine a new discovery in some long forgotten cave in Palestine. There, the desiccated remains of a man in his early thirties are found, and reliably dated to the first century AD. Enough is preserved, however, to show that he was tortured, including signs of puncture wounds around his head. He was apparently crucified from evidence of trauma to his hands and feet, and there are indications that his side was pierced by a weapon of some sort. With the corpse is a document, written by someone who claimed to be the man's twin. It describes a whole set of events that were apparently miraculous, but were actually very sophisticated magic tricks. Like explanations in the notes left by the great Harry Houdini, we find out how the illusions were performed. The subterfuge culminated when the writer took the place of his brother after his execution, and encouraged his followers to believe in him as their resurrected leader.

As unlikely as this might be, such a find is not impossible. The Dead Sea Scrolls were preserved for the better part of two millennia, and some gnostic traditions speak of the twin brother of Jesus.[15] If this happens, it would shake my faith, precisely because it challenges the actual resurrection of Christ. I believe in this as a historical reality, and as such, I can envision evidence that does or does not support it. My hypothetical discovery in the desert is an example of the latter. If future archaeologists make such a find, we would have to admit that Christ was not raised from the dead. In that case, I can only agree with Paul that we Christians are among those who should be "most pitied," as he states in 1 Corinthians 15:19.

There is, however, another position. You can say that the situation I describe is an issue solely because I am resorting to a "God of the gaps." Up until the time the telltale corpse is found, I attribute the resurrection of Christ to God because I have no other explanation. I find the discovery disturbing because I see him only as the one who fills any gaps in my knowledge. Recall that earlier in the chapter, I mentioned that some Christians want to avoid "God of the gaps" arguments at all costs. Because of this, they have a solution to my problem. Namely, I should not worry about the evidence I describe, since after all, archaeologists were bound to make such a discovery sooner or later. Our faith is questioned by this find, so these Christians

---

15. Elaine Pagels, *The Gnostic Gospels* (New York: Random House, 1979).

might argue, only by our failure to anticipate it. It is our lack of imagination that keeps us from understanding that everything we observe can ultimately have a "naturalistic" explanation. Once I realize this, the "tomb that is not empty" challenges only the "God of the gaps," not the one true God in whom we should believe.

Following this line of reasoning, we would have to conclude that our beliefs should be based, instead, on non-empirical arguments that purport to show, for example, the logical necessity of a Supreme Being. I am not denying the utility of such arguments, and since they can be cast in the form of "proofs," their potential for "irrefutability" is very appealing. However, wholly restricting ourselves to such an approach does come with a price. For one thing, this only gets us to "mere theism"—the God of the philosophers. Yet it does remove an awkwardness Christians face in the scientific academy—no need to posit a supernatural explanation for a physical effect, for natural explanations for all that we presently consider supernatural will be eventually uncovered.

But, now this is beginning to sound like Gould's NOMA, and therein lies the crux of the issue. We might rightly object to the insinuation that our faith is subjective fantasy, as the realm of our "magisterium" might suggest. However, if it is simply based on philosophy, which is equally distinct from scientific "reality," the veracity of our concrete belief in the Gospels becomes irrelevant. It no longer matters if God raised Christ from the dead, as their writers believed, or was replaced by his twin, since the quality of our logic is more important that the strength of the evidence for our beliefs.

It is clear that such a faith would not be the kind of Christianity to which Paul and those who followed him bore witness. This is why it is so important that the preponderance of historical evidence to date supports the reality of the events on which Christians base their hope for salvation. The details are beyond the scope of the present discussion, but to quote the historian F. F. Bruce, "The historicity of Christ is as axiomatic for an unbiased historian as the historicity of Julius Caesar."[16] If anything, the ability to formulate a scenario that could refute such a claim, and see no evidence to date for it,

16. F. F. Bruce, *The New Testament Documents: Are They Reliable?* (Grand Rapids: Eerdmans, 2003).

adds to the persuasiveness of the argument that Jesus Christ was who he claimed to be as the Son of God.

Christians should thus not be afraid of the charge of engaging in "God of the gaps" thinking. Instead, we should see it as a means of challenging "methodological naturalism," i. e., that only natural explanations for what we observe in the physical world constitute science, and by implication, the supernatural does not exist (which is "metaphysical naturalism"). The incarnation itself demonstrates once and for all that God has bridged the separation between the supernatural and natural world. We appreciate how extraordinary this is, because we have both a "scientific" knowledge of standard human reproduction and the consequences of crucifixion, and the historical record of the singular birth, death, and resurrection of Christ. Consequently, Christians should not be so quick to deny the possibility that other "gaps" are not voids in our knowledge. I am clearly not advocating, especially as a scientist, the idea of ascribing anything we do not easily understand to a supernatural agent. However, the gaps we perceive *could* be indicators of profound truths about God, as manifest in the physical world that he created. While methodological naturalism is a good starting assumption for scientific research, adhering to it at all costs may very well blind us to those truths.

How does all of this inform on redeeming the mind as it involves the practice and teaching of science? In the physical sciences, the claim that our universe appears to reflect the work of a "designer" is not immediately dismissed as beyond the pale. As described earlier, the arguments made by Gonzales and Richardson in *The Privileged Planet* are rooted in mainstream research. Indeed, an article entitled "Anthropic Reasoning" appeared in *Science* magazine in 2005 by two prominent astronomers, Mario Livio of the Space Telescope Science Institute and Martin J. Rees of the University of Cambridge. Like Gonzales and Richardson, they consider as "generic" certain requirements for any form of life to exist: "galaxies, stars, and (probably) planets had to form; nucleosynthesis in stars had to give rise to atoms such as carbon, oxygen, and iron; and these atoms had to be in a stable environment where they could combine to form the molecules of life."[17] They are clearly a necessity for intelligent life on earth, hence the name "anthropic."

17. Mario Livio and Martin J. Rees, "Anthropic Reasoning," *Science* 309 (2005): 1022.

Livio and Rees comment on various reasons why some physicists are hostile to this approach. They put it as follows.

> [A]nthropic reasoning seems to point to a fundamental limitation of physics—even the "end of physics." But this objection is, in our opinion, a purely psychological one. Physicists would like, above all else, to discover a uniquely self-consistent set of equations that determines all microphysical constants, and the recipe for the big bang. They therefore hope that future theories will reveal that all physical parameters are uniquely determined. But there is no reason why physical reality should be structured according to their preferences. It is good that many physicists are motivated to seek a theory that uniquely derives all fundamental numbers and constants, but they may be doomed to failure.[18]

Livio and Rees thus point out the very real possibility that a theory that uniquely determines all physical parameters may never be found. They do not mince words in claiming that to think otherwise may very well be an act of faith. Following this line of reasoning, the assertion that science will fill all present "gaps" in our knowledge, and thus leave no "room" for God, takes on the trappings of a religious creed. Under these circumstances, it is not unreasonable for a physicist to believe in a "designer" behind the universe, and yet be "true" to science.

When it comes to the biological sciences, however, there appears to be a reluctance to consider the idea of a "designer" at their roots. It may very well be that this reflects, in part, the different origins of the biological and physical sciences. In exploring this idea, it is helpful to recall the example of Paul at the Aeropagus. There, he took great pains to use terminology that would not be foreign to his listeners to ensure proper communication with them. Similarly, we should allow the possibility that the different perspectives held in the physical and biological sciences could be aggravated by seemingly identical terms, but with dissimilar meanings because they did not develop in the same way. We may think that this sort of communication problem is more common to the humanities, but it can arise in the sciences as well.

As an example, the recent controversy over ID has brought to the fore the question of what is meant by words like "theory" and even

---

18. Ibid.

"science" itself. To provide a context for discussing this, I begin with an assertion made by the great British playwright George Bernard Shaw. He is reputed to have once said that America and England are two countries separated by a common language. There are many cases that support his claim. Among the more serious ones, consider an incident that occurred during the end of World War II. The last major German offensive happened in December of 1944, and it became known as the "Battle of the Bulge." To cause confusion behind American lines, some English-speaking German soldiers dressed as GIs infiltrated them. They were easily caught, however, when they did such things as ask where to get "petrol." The German infiltrators did indeed know English, but of the "wrong" kind.

A personal motivation for thinking that there might be a similar problem in the sciences was an experience I had not too long ago. I was giving an introductory talk on nuclear fusion, the area of my expertise, to some students in my institution. In an attempt to show my erudition in the history of science as well as science itself, I made the following statement. "The term 'fission' was originally coined by biologists to describe what happened to cells when they divide. It was then adapted by scientists to name the process by which heavy nuclei break up." I realized what I said as soon as the words left my lips. It was too late, however, judging from the smirks that quickly appeared on the faces of the listeners. All I could do was admit that I was not even going to try to get myself out of that one, and simply went on with my lecture.

The issue is not to debate whether or not biology is "real" science, my exceedingly embarrassing slip notwithstanding. Rather, it is that the same word is associated with phenomena that appear to be superficially similar, but with very different implications concerning its functional definition. I am not suggesting that the ongoing difficulties over issues like ID are just a matter of semantics. However, I do firmly believe that any resolution depends critically on establishing a terminology that is the same in both form and function.

An understanding of "fission" in biology, for example, is generally cast in terms of providing the most accurate description possible of the process. From the first time cells were identified by van Leeuwenhoek, biologists have amassed a tremendous amount of information about them. We now know exactly what is required for cells to fission. Mitosis first requires the duplication of chromosomes and the synthesis of the proteins that form the so-called "mitotic spindle." The chromosomes thicken and coil, and the nuclear membrane disintegrates. The chromatid pairs that constitute the chromosomes are pulled to opposite ends of the cell by the spindle fibers. The fission occurs after the nuclear membranes re-form around the separated chromosomes, and the cytoplasm of the original cell divides to create two new cells.[19]

In contrast, an understanding of "fission" in physics is not reflected in the details of its description alone. Rather, it is based on the ability to calculate under what conditions fission will occur. To quote Bohr and Mottelson from their classic text on nuclear structure, "fissionability depends on the ratio of the Coulomb energy (proportional to the square of the total charge Z divided by the cube root of the mass number A) to the surface energy (proportional to the mass number to the 2/3 power)."[20]

Increasing biological knowledge is generally construed in terms of *adding* more details concerning a particular object of study. Understanding fission means that you can put the steps prophase, metaphase, anaphase, telophase, and interphase in the right sequence and describe what happens in each of these phases. In physics, on the other hand, comprehension is gauged by the *simplifications* uncovered by research, and the basic knowledge that discovering them implies. In this context, typical is the conclusion, also from Bohr and Mottelson, that "the lifetime of spontaneous fission depends on the parameter Z^2/A."[21]

The semantic dissimilarity between biological and physical sciences could be a reflection of a fundamental difference in the way the disciplines developed historically. The great physicist Richard Feynman once described the challenge faced by those of us in the physical sciences: "Suppose that physics, or rather nature, is considered analogous to a great game of chess with millions of pieces in it, and we are trying to discover the laws by which the pieces move."[22] Physicists have been remarkably successful in discovering these laws and making the equally amazing discovery that there are a relatively small number of them. The few "laws of nature"

19. *The New Encyclopedia Britannica,* 15th ed., s.v. "Mitosis."
20. Aage Bohr and Ben R. Mottelson, *Nuclear Structure, Volume I* (New York: W. A Benjamin, 1969), 205.
21. Ibid.
22. Richard Feynman, *The Character of Physical Law* (Cambridge, MA: MIT Press, 1967).

can describe a whole panoply of phenomena, from the behavior of subatomic particles to the motions of galaxies. This purportedly led Albert Einstein to claim that the most incomprehensible thing about the universe is that it is comprehensible. Mathematics is the key to this "comprehensibility" for physicists, and from such a realization, concluding that there is an "intelligence" that causes this to be is not too hard for many of them.

Contrast this to what is often cited as foundational to biology as a modern science, which is described in great detail in Gould's *The Structure of Evolutionary Theory*. This massive book is a treasure trove of very illuminating history, and thus serves as a window into the differences between the biological and physical sciences. Modern biology began, to use Gould's words, when Charles Darwin "rejected the traditional claims of quantitative physical science to represent the apotheosis of sophistication, and awarded high honor to his own discipline of natural history and evolutionary biology, as embodied in the gnarly and meandering icon of the luxuriantly, but contingently, branching tree of life."[23]

It should be noted that contemporary science has become so cross-disciplinary that the distinction between the physical and life sciences is often very blurred. Many universities no longer have single biology departments, but divide them according to subfields like biochemistry, molecular biology, biophysics, and bioengineering, as if they were separate disciplines. In these examples, the experimental and theoretical approaches often differ little from those in physics and chemistry. For the present discussion, biology is used in the sense of evolutionary biology, that is, the subject having the basic characteristics first articulated by Darwin.

Here we have perhaps the most fundamental problem with "science" as a term that appears to have two distinct meanings. Gould suggests that the true revolution of Darwin was to include the narrative approach as a perfectly appropriate, and even superior way of doing science. In a section of his book entitled "Darwin's Geological Need and Kelvin's Odious Spectre," Gould describes what he calls "one of the most arrogant documents in the history of science—a one-paragraph paper (with appended calculation) boldly entitled "The 'Doctrine of Uniformity' in Geology Briefly Refuted."[24]

---

23. Stephen Jay Gould, *The Structure of Evolutionary Theory*, 1334.
24. Ibid., 493.

Briefly, the paper was the attempt by William Thomson, the future Lord Kelvin, to show that we can calculate an upper bound on the age of the earth by how long it would take our planet to cool from an initially molten state. He ultimately came up with an age of ten to thirty million years, at least for the duration of a solid upper crust. Kelvin used this as a demonstration that there simply was not enough time for small effects to accumulate in sufficient quantity for the gradual, uniform change required by Darwin's theory of evolution.

This was in 1866, however, before the discovery of radioactivity. This was a new source of heat, unknown to Kelvin, which meant that you could not deduce the age of the earth by present measurements of its interior heat. Kelvin's arrogance was thus groundless, and this has been often cited as justifying the angry feelings Gould claims Darwin to have had about the pretensions of mathematical physics and celestial mechanics to superior status over natural history among the sciences.

There are a couple of ironies here. First, even tens of millions of years was considered a very long time for many supporters of gradualism in the nineteenth century. Furthermore, the idea of gradualism itself has been called into question by many modern admirers of Darwin, including Gould himself. The key point is that Darwin's main contribution, to continue quoting Gould, is to contrast "the dull repetitiveness of planetary cycling (despite the elegance and simplicity of its quantitative expression) with the gutsy glory of rich diversity on life's ever rising and expanding tree."[25]

I might not necessarily appreciate Gould's characterization of physics. I cannot argue with his basic sentiments, however, as they do echo what I wrote at the beginning of this chapter. Concerning what he says about biology, this may be able to explain a particular conundrum in that field. On the one hand, you have writers like Gould and others who provide such critiques of Darwin's original work that only a vague outline remains in the alternatives they propose. Gould, for example, challenges Darwin's gradualism with his aphorism that "stasis is data" according to the fossil record.[26] He is very forthright when he states that Darwinists know, "in their heart of hearts," what a "leap of faith into the enabling power of geological time" they are taking, rather than recognizing it as a

25. Ibid., 1334.
26. Ibid., 790.

"bankrupt argument" for macroevolution, based on the "small inputs [of] microevolutionary adaptation."[27]

The key point is not the accuracy of Gould's claims. Rather, it is the fact that he can use such strong and colorful language in his critique, and yet assert his emphatic support for evolutionary theory as established by Darwin. To do otherwise would seem to be a challenge to science itself, as much of the recent rhetoric over teaching alternatives to Darwinism might suggest. This is in spite of the fact that authors like Gould point out its flaws and decry the poor quality of the treatment of evolution in widely-used textbooks.[28]

To help understand this, let us consider another word, "theory," that seems to have two very different connotations. Theories are treated in the physical and biological sciences in very different ways. For the physical scientist, a theory is the best means that we have at the present time to explain a particular set of phenomena. Its validity is based on the predictive power of the calculations we perform. The very fact that the physical sciences are quantitative disciplines also gives us an inherent sense of the limitations of our theories. This is why physics is rife with wisecracks like "the terms that are too hard to calculate are assumed not to contribute."

As an example, consider a bumper sticker that was inspired by the recent ID controversy. It reads, "What's next, gravity?" While the intent behind such a slogan is clear, the irony is that in fact, we do not have a complete theory of gravitation. We can *calculate* the "dull repetitiveness of planetary cycling," to use Gould's unkind words, but how to reconcile Einstein's classical theory of general relativity with quantum mechanics is still very much an open question. Since the big shakeup in physics that relativity and quantum mechanics caused in the last century, challenges to theories are not as much a concern to physical scientists as one might think. In that sense, the bumper sticker should not be shocking to them. What is next on the agenda is indeed gravity, as it has been for quite a while.

"Theory" seems to have a very different meaning in the biological sciences. There, it appears to connote more of a conceptual framework for the field. In that sense, there is indeed an overarching "theory of biology" that traces its origins to Darwin. As mentioned earlier, he sought to establish his narrative approach to natural history and

27. Ibid., 1294.
28. Ibid., 577.

evolutionary biology as being every bit as scientific as the quantitative physical sciences. This is why questioning evolutionary theory, as so used, is equated with questioning science.

For the physical scientist, it would be equivalent to questioning the validity of mathematics. We do not have an equivalent "theory of physics," but we do believe that without mathematics, we would not have a scientific discipline. If this conceptual framework is what we mean by "theory," we can appreciate the concerns of biologists. If this is the case, however, it points out the very different implications the term has in the physical and biological sciences. This must be appreciated if there is to be a common language for communicating between the disciplines, at least as far as what is meant by their respective "theoretical" bases.

Given the differences in what the term implies, this might be another case where a heuristic approach might be helpful. Perhaps we can introduce a new term, like "principle" into the discussion of evolution in biology. If used instead of "theory," it might sidestep all of the difficulties this term's connotations engender. In the physical sciences, "principles" have something of the flavor of conceptual frameworks. The "Uncertainty Principle" in physics tells us that we cannot know the position and momentum of an object with arbitrary accuracy. It is not a theory as such, but reflects a deep, and so far apparently immutable, characteristic of nature.

Instead of ID as a *theoretical* alternative to evolution, in that case, perhaps we can substitute it with the "Design Principle." Its basis would be the assertion that what looks poorly designed at first glance is not really so after deeper scrutiny. It could be used to challenge, for example, the old "chestnut" that the human eye is "wired backwards." In fact, recently analyses have shown this is not necessarily the case for an organ that has to process a time sequence of images.[29] We can contrast this with the "Evolution Principle." The idea here is that what we see in biological systems is not well-designed, but "kluged together" as you would expect from the "blind" operation of natural selection. "The Panda's Thumb" is not just the name of a famous essay by Gould,[30] but has become almost iconic for this point of view.

29. George Ayoub, "On the Design of the Vertebrate Retina," *Origins and Design* 17 (1996): 19.

30. Stephen J. Gould, *The Panda's Thumb: More Reflections in Natural History* (New York: W. W. Norton, 1980).

An advantage of introducing such new terms is to "give ID a rest," as one might say colloquially. Given all the emotions surrounding it, this should not be underrated. Furthermore, it would allow everybody to use the same methodologies to do their research. In the past, ID has been criticized for its encouragement of a "God did it, look no further" attitude. Interestingly, the "Evolutionary Principle" can also stop science in a similar way. It is admittedly a very unlikely scenario, but one could conceive of a biologist deciding that a "kluge is a kluge." In other words, if a structure obviously looks like it was thrown together for a particular function, there is no deeper reason for its apparently "poor" design. The "Design Principle" advocate, however, might very well argue that further investigation is warranted to see if some less obvious functionality is being missed. Seeing how such arguments can go either way, these possibilities should warn us not to prejudge the behavior of scientists based on their philosophical inclinations. Rather, we should see what they actually do in the laboratory and the field.

It might help us appreciate why the philosophy behind the science is important, if we return to the difference in mindset between many biological and physical scientists. One way to summarize this is to comment on a recent book on evolution by two biologists, Kirschner and Gerhart, entitled *The Plausibility of Life: Resolving Darwin's Dilemma*.[31] It was reviewed in a recent issue of *American Scientist* by a fellow biologist who criticized the title, but not for the reason you might expect.[32] The reviewer began as follows: "Is life plausible? Well, it's more than plausible, it has actually happened!" This is the kind of thinking that explains why the authors did not call their book "The *Probability* of Life," and it suggests that the view of science many biologists have that began with Darwin persists to this day.

Physicists can tell you where a planet will be with high probability after the elapse of a specific amount of time. This is "dull" to biologists, Gould seems to suggest, because once a plausible argument for planetary motion is described, such calculations are not necessary to make it more believable. To the biologists having this viewpoint, *probability* arguments, as physicists might craft them, are not persuasive. Rather, the original *plausibility* argument is more

31. Marc W. Kirschner and John C. Gerhart, *The Plausibility of Life: Resolving Darwin's Dilemma* (New Haven, CT: Yale University Press, 2005).
32. Massimo Pigliucci, "Have We Solved Darwin's Dilemma?," *American Scientist* 94 (2006): 272.

convincing, because only such a narrative form can capture such things as "the gnarly and meandering icon of the luxuriantly, but contingently, branching tree of life," to quote Gould once more. This is not to argue, by any means, that physics is science and biology is not, or vice-versa. Rather, we must first be sensitive to differences between the disciplines in their understanding of what science is. As we have seen, they have their origins in the different ways biology and physics developed historically. These dissimilarities continue to manifest themselves in the semantics of their terminology and the way each is practiced.

Suppose there is broader recognition among physicists and biologists that such issues indeed exist. Coming to terms with them can then serve as a paradigm for addressing more visibly contentious topics like ID. As in the case with biology and physics, an appreciation of the nuances in what constitutes science could then be the basis of a constructive dialog.

A Common Solution

What are the implications of trying to achieve a common understanding of science for redeeming the mind? It could be argued that this might be all "academic," since a discussion of the meaning of science has little to do with the success of academia in the practical part of its educational mission. According to Malik, "The sciences are flourishing as never before, and may they keep on flourishing and exploding and discovering!"[33]

At one level, Malik is right. You can quite competently design the next generation of laser scanners for supermarket checkout counters based on the formalisms of quantum mechanics, even if you do not appreciate all of its metaphysical difficulties. Similarly, you can develop a new vaccine for the next flu season, appreciating full well the tendency of the influenza virus to mutate, without accepting all of the philosophical implications of evolutionary theory. As James Gould, a professor of ecology and evolutionary biology at Princeton University, has put it, "If you think about it, does it really matter whether you think intelligent design or evolution is what accounts

---

33. See page 60 in chapter 2.

for the diversity of life on earth if you're going to be a banker, or a lawyer, or a doctor?"[34]

For the Christian, such issues do matter, in that the way we think about them informs on how we consider the deeper questions of meaning and purpose for our lives. It is here that the two tasks converge. At first glance, the work of redeeming the soul and redeeming the mind may seem to require very different approaches. In both, however, there is a common need to communicate, whether it concerns the truth of the book of nature or the Book that tells us of how our souls can be saved. Both come from the same God, and both reveal him in a unique way. To meet this challenge, we can learn much from the heuristic tactics of Paul. As he was sensitive to the mindset of those he wished to reach, so should we be where God, in his wisdom, has placed each of us.

Discussion Questions

1. How are heuristic examples useful?
2. What are limitations of the heuristic approach?
3. How might the heuristic approach look within your own discipline?
4. In what ways is first-century Athens similar to twenty-first-century America? In what ways are they different?
5. How does the example of Paul at the Areopagus inform on the two tasks?
6. Why is a "common language" important in the two tasks?
7. What human tendencies complicate communication in any discipline?
8. What may limit the acceptance of concepts like a "designer" in the sciences?

---

34. Quoted by Brett Thomlinson in "Where Science Meets Religion," *Princeton Alumni Weekly* 106 (2006): 20.

7

THE TEXT'S THE THING: REFLECTIONS FROM THE HUMANITIES

JOHN NORTH

"Who is it who can tell me who I am?"
—King Lear

"God's my life! . . . I have had a most rare vision."
—Bottom in *A Midsummer Night's Dream*

Sir, why are you a Christian?" Kelly asked, standing an awkward six feet away from my desk. Two months from graduating at the top end of her computer science class, she was taking Shakespeare as an option. After eight weeks of lectures in the comfortable anonymity of a large class, she had come by this morning unannounced to ask a class-related question as a ploy to see if I was approachable enough for her to ask the one biggest, most real question from the depths of her private distress. Knowing that her father was Chinese and her mother Dutch, I vaguely wondered about her impassive expression. My next lecture was only twenty minutes away, but the urgency of this question had to be answered in the moment. "Be ready always to give an answer to every man that asketh you a reason of the hope that is in you with meekness and fear" (1 Peter 3:15, KJV), says Peter. So as Kelly sat in sober silence I spoke of my lifelong need for daily forgiveness, of the compassion of the Savior of my soul, of his incarnation and resurrection and ascension on my behalf, of the Lord who is as infinitely minute in his love and awareness as he is great in his creating and sustaining of billions of stars, the "micro" as well as the "macro" Jesus Christ. Then I gave her that excellent book, *3:16 Bible Texts Illuminated*, by Professor Donald Knuth of Stanford,[1] whom some know as the father of computing in North America, and who in that little volume provides an explanation of every chapter 3 and verse 16 in the Bible, with accompanying illustrations by calligraphers from around the world. The volume focuses on John 3:16, which as Professor Knuth points out is the best-known verse in the Bible. I suggested she speak to the Lord herself in the quiet of her room, and left for class. The next day Kelly appeared at the door, her face now glowing with vitality and "the peace that passes understanding." Why have you come to Christ, Kelly? Her reply: "Sir, I'm a bad girl." Her final paper for that Shakespeare class closed with the directness of St. Paul, "He that believeth not is condemned already" (John 3:18, KJV).

Kelly had asked King Lear's question, "Who is it who can tell me who I am?" Overcome with shame, she echoed Lear's cry, "I am bound / Upon a wheel of fire, that mine own tears / Do scald like molten lead."[2] And now here she was, like Bottom in *A Midsummer Night's Dream* (you may remember him as the egoistical tradesman who when lost in the forest at night had been found, cuddled, protected, and admired, ass of a man that he was, by Titania, Queen of the Air), proclaiming in awe, "God's my life." Many voices were telling Kelly who she was: she was caught between two cultures; she was a computer geek; and (most shrill voice of all) she was an immoral undergraduate woman. Voices she could no longer ignore or deny. Until at last she had heard the voice of the Lover of her soul, saying, "Come unto me, all ye that labour and are heavy laden, and I will give you rest . . . unto your souls. . . . There is therefore now no condemnation to them which are in Christ Jesus" (Matt. 11:28–29; Rom. 8:1, KJV). Here was a voice telling her who she was, a voice she

---

1. Donald Knuth, *3:16 Bible Texts Illuminated* (Madison, WI: AR Editions, 1990).
2. *King Lear*, ed. Russell Fraser (New York: The New American Library, 1963), 4.7.46–48. References are to act, scene, and line.

ached to hear, again in the language of Shakespeare, whose Titania, Queen of the Air, a thinly disguised Christ figure, says to Bottom: "I do love thee: therefore go with me, / . . . And I will purge thy mortal grossness so / That thou shalt like an airy spirit go."[3]

"For proud and rebellious and self-sufficient man . . . to be brought to his knees and to his tears before the actual majesty and grace and power of Jesus Christ is the greatest event that can happen to any man. . . . And those who are engaged in mediating this event, the evangelists, are the supreme heralds of God," says Charles Malik.[4] Our Lord so calls us all, and fits us as university professors spending our lives in communicating with young people at this critical stage in their lives, the time when they are separating from home, choosing a spouse and a profession, discovering their gifts, developing their worldview. They read our souls more eagerly than they read our minds. We in the Humanities have many resources for our fellows who are asking, as did King Lear, "Who am I?" Our students' questions include: "What is worthy of devoting my life to? What am I worth, and to whom? Where is excitement and vitality and intensity of relationships to be found?" But most of all, "Where is a beloved who loves me?" Last year a student group asked of what my life consisted: "The same as yours, a passionate searching out of intimacy, beauty, and understanding, in that order. The extent to which I find each is in some curious way the extent of my knowing Jesus Christ, who is the Way, the Truth, and the Life. Communing with him I exclaim, in the words of Shakespeare's character Bottom when his friends marvel at what has happened to him, 'God's my life! . . . I have had a most rare vision. . . . I am to discourse wonders. . . . I will tell you everything, right as it fell out.'"[5]

Over the years the most focused, boldness-requiring of the two tasks for me has been to win the souls of my students and colleagues for Jesus Christ. Years ago I remember walking to campus and being prompted to pray, "Lord, it has been a long time since I have spoken of Jesus to anyone here. . . ." At the same moment I saw half a block away an approaching student. As she came closer I recognized her from one of my classes. We met, stopped, and in ten minutes I recounted to her the ways of my Savior. We parted, I astonished

---

3. *A Midsummer Night's Dream* (Cambridge: Cambridge University Press, 1949), 3.1.147–52. References are to act, scene, and line.

4. See pages 58–59 in chapter 2.

5. *A Midsummer Night's Dream*, 3.1.147–52.

at the responsiveness of the Holy Spirit. When hearts are won, the fullness of joy and depth of fellowship far exceeds that rising from any academic accomplishments.

In fact, for me it has often followed the winning of minds. Over the years, to present the abundant Christian content of English literature in a matter-of-fact rather than in a coercive or defensive way has become almost routine. This is a winning of the minds. For instance, to put Jesus' statement, "As Moses lifted up the serpent in the wilderness, even so must the Son of man be lifted up. . . . And I, if I be lifted up from the earth, will draw all men unto me" (John 3:14; 12:32, KJV) in the context of the Hebrew Moses putting a serpent of brass on a pole (see Num. 21:9, KJV) and of the Greek caduceus (the common medical symbol) is quite straightforward. The linking of Christian, Hebrew, and Greek cultures both takes the sting out of the issue, and enriches our Lord's assertion for the class. To observe that in Christianity as well as in Jewish, Hindu, and Greek cultures one of the strongest metaphors for knowing God is sexual "knowledge" brings light into their eyes and attentive physical stillness.

Only this past week, following the example set by Donald Knuth, who each year at term end invites his students to ask any question, within or beyond the course materials, I myself gave that same invitation one month into term, inviting them to ask in class, or in my office, or by e-mail, or by phone, day or night. So Carol, a fourth-year math student, dropped by my office yesterday afternoon and opened with, "Sir, how did you come to teach Shakespeare the way you do?" Earlier in the morning the Shakespeare class discussion had been about *King Richard the Third*, Clarence's nightmare of drowning, finding himself in hell, and facing the accusations of his life of sinfulness. This nightmare is followed in the next scenes by Clarence's prayer of confession and repentance, then his testimony of the forgiveness of "our dear Redeemer" to men sent to murder him. His testimony of the gospel of forgiveness is echoed by the dying King Edward IV in the opening scene of the next act. Carol affirmed, "Yes, sir, what you teach is simply the detail of the play, but others don't teach that kind of thing." She listened to my confession of Christ, then went off to work in the campus coffee shop, our discussion to be picked up next week.

Winning others' souls can only follow the winning of my own. That monumental ongoing battle I fight on several fronts. One is my habitual congregational worship of Christ. Another is daily prayer and Scripture reading with my wife, the only certain way to deal with lurking resentments before sleeping ("Let not the sun go down upon your wrath," that astute traveling Roman Jew Paul urges in Eph. 4:26, KJV). Yet another is disciplined service, in teaching Christian formation classes at our church or in local hospital chaplaincy work. Spur-of-the-moment courage to respond to colleagues and students like Kelly and Carol is especially difficult. Every new occasion is an unexpected and momentary confrontation with hell, a leap into the void. That courage has increased when with a hungry heart I have searched out soul food in books like those of Paul Tournier, the Swiss psychiatrist, who tells of the healing of patients' souls in his writings *Escape from Loneliness, The Person Reborn, The Strong and the Weak, Guilt and Grace, A Place for You,* and *The Meaning of Persons*; in commentaries and biblical expositions like those of Helmut Thielicke, the German pastor and theologian, writing *How to Believe Again, Freedom of the Christian Man, I Believe: The Christian's Creed, Between God and Satan,* and *Being a Christian When the Chips Are Down*; in sociological analyses such as the French Jacques Ellul's *Violence, The Meaning of the City, Money and Power,* and *The New Demons*; in handbooks such as the InterVarsity Press's *Hard Sayings of the Bible*; or the poetry of Gerard Manley Hopkins ("I am soft sift in an hourglass . . ."[6]).

For many years, one of my greatest consolations was knowing, as a result of reading Tournier's case histories, that were the sufferings of life ever to become unbearable, for a thousand dollars I could go to Switzerland and pour out my grief to a Christian who would always listen, never condemn, always understand, always fellowship. To know that such a man lived and worshiped and cared, and where he could be found, as it turned out, was enough, so I never did have to make the journey. When he reached his nineties I had the privilege of meeting him, in Belfast, standing by his chair unable to speak a syllable, and hearing him say "Write, it will be easier." I did, only needing to say "Thank you, Paul." Could any of my students gain similar sustenance from me, Lord?

---

6. Gerard Manley Hopkins, "The Wreck of the Deutschland," in *The Poems of Gerard Manley Hopkins*, ed. W. H. Gardner and N. H. Mackenzie (London: Oxford University Press, 1967), 27.

One of the most consoling ways of saving my soul, and yet also a discipline requiring me to bare this soul, is to establish regular Christian fellowship with a variety of individuals across campus. Several years ago a colleague from another department phoned at 1:00 a.m.: "John, sorry to bother you so late, but I know that sometimes you have unusual folk stay at your place. Could I stay with you overnight?" Sure. "Do you mind coming to pick me up?" Of course I'll come, where? "At the jail. I have no money, no glasses, no wallet, only my shorts, shirt, tennis shoes, and only this one phone call." I'll be there in fifteen minutes.

It was the beginning of a rare intimacy with a fellow believer in marital difficulty, an intimacy that has enlarged to include his now teenage children, and has strengthened during the past six years rather than diminished. We share each other's griefs and joys in a friendship that I could not have imagined between men of such different temperaments and interests. It all began that night of his humiliating phone call, when he heard a familiar voice saying what he had scarce dared hope for: "You are my friend, come home with me." Earlier that evening he had heard other voices: his wife calling him a brute; the police mocking him and putting him needlessly on public display as a university professor who had kicked his wife; a court order telling him he could not return home.

I first took university classes seriously in my fourth year of undergraduate studies at the University of British Columbia, reading S. T. Coleridge's "The Rime of the Ancient Mariner." Until then I had been more caught up in my girlfriend, my part-time job, the struggles of separating from my family home and of discovering my own way in life. Then one day everything came together when I read Coleridge's seminal poem in our Romantic Poetry class with Professor Craig Millar. In that poem Coleridge records his conversion from Unitarianism to Christ, in the persona of the mariner. You may remember the tale: the mariner had idly shot an albatross while on a voyage. Calamities followed, until, he records, "instead of the cross the Albatross about my neck was hung"[7] by his accusing shipmates. Both he and they recognized that he had been an unwitting participant in the crucifixion. He tells of finding

---

7. S. T. Coleridge, "The Rime of the Ancient Mariner," in *The Poems of Samuel Taylor Coleridge*, ed. E. H. Coleridge (London, Oxford University Press, 1960), part 2, lines 141–42, p. 191.

relief from the anguish of his guilt only when, seeing sea-snakes ("slimy things that swam upon a slimy sea") rear up so that flakes of phosphorescent light fell off them, "my kind saint took pity on me, and I blessed them unaware. / The selfsame moment I could pray; / And from my neck so free / The Albatross fell off, and sank / Like lead into the sea."[8] In other words, when he was enabled to see the beauty of Christ. The poem ends with lines so poignant they are worth repeating at length:

> O Wedding Guest! This soul hath been
> Alone on a wide wide sea:
> So lonely 'twas, that God himself
> Scarce seemed there to be.
>
> O sweeter than the marriage feast,
> 'Tis sweeter far to me,
> To walk together to the kirk
> With a goodly company!—
>
> To walk together to the kirk,
> And all together pray,
> While each to his great Father bends,
> Old men, and babes, and loving friends
> And youths and maidens gay!
>
> Farewell, farewell! But this I tell
> To thee, thou Wedding Guest!
> He prayeth well, who loveth well
> Both man and bird and beast.
>
> He prayeth best who loveth best,
> All things both great and small,
> For the dear God who loveth us,
> He made and loveth all.[9]

I knew that the gospel records Jesus saying, "As Moses lifted up the serpent in the wilderness, even so must the Son of man be lifted up" (John 3:14, KJV); and even at twenty-one I knew the comfort and peace and renewal of Christian congregational worship. Suddenly here I

---

8. Ibid., part 2, lines 288–91, p. 198.
9. Ibid., part 2, lines 597–617, p. 208–9.

was reading one of the great poets who had put into words my own life experience. That poem somehow validated my being. I asked an eager question, then another, and another in rapid succession—I, one of the many passive observers in class who never asked questions. In a moment I was hooked on English literature and have never turned back. The mariner put into words my own loneliness, my own route to peace, my own life of worship, and especially my own call to evangelism, of which I was then only vaguely aware. The mariner describes all of us as called to evangelize—a hermit, startled by the mariner's manner, asks with intensity (as Kelly and others have since asked me):

> "Say quick," quoth he, "I bid thee say—
> What manner of man art thou?"
>
> Forthwith this frame of mine was wrenched
> With a woeful agony,
> Which forced me to begin my tale;
> And then it left me free.
>
> Since then, at an uncertain hour,
> That agony returns;
> And till my ghastly tale is told,
> This heart within me burns.
>
> I pass, like night, from land to land;
> I have strange power of speech;
> That moment that his face I see,
> I know the man that must hear me:
> To him my tale I teach.[10]

During the intervening years I have become increasingly aware how precisely Coleridge's voice describes my own inner state from day to day. I have discovered that most of the canon of English literature as well as many non-canonical works have been written by self-confessed Christians, men and women using this art form to glorify God in carrying out the two tasks of saving souls and minds. Wonderful that my profession has required me to instruct so many thousands of students in the works of Tennyson, Browning, Shakespeare, Chaucer, Milton, Herrick, the Bronte sisters, Jane

10. Ibid., part 2, lines 576–590, p. 208.

Austen, John Ruskin, Charles Dickens, T. S. Eliot, e.e. Cummings—all these Christ-confessors. Even the despairing search of Franz Kafka ("The Hunger Artist," *The Trial*, "Metamorphosis," "The Country Doctor") and Samuel Beckett (*Waiting for Godot, Krapp's Last Tape*) provides parables of our souls' longing for God.

Hearing the Voice of God among Many Voices

Walking down the hospital corridor late one evening, having been called to the bedside of a dying eighty-five-year-old, in his youth a World War II frogman in the Royal Navy, I passed a stretcher on which Mr. Fujikama was being wheeled into a private room. Hello, Mr. Fujikama. What are you doing here? "I have cancer of the spine, Mr. North. Serious. What are you doing here?"—all in his gentle Japanese accent, as he folded his hands and attempted a bow while lying flat on his back. Mr. Fujikama had been the high school math teacher as well as orchestra and choir leader of our three sons. Born and educated in Japan, he had come to Canada and spent his career teaching high school. With a marked accent, a rare gentleness of spirit, and always elegant manners, Mr. Fujikama had been one of our sons' favorite teachers. I replied that I was a volunteer chaplain, that I found this spending of the evenings with the sick and dying to be a thought-provoking and peace-giving balance to my days spent with late adolescents in the fullness of their lives.

Several days later as I was passing down the palliative care hallway, called to see another man in the last hours of a cancer death, I noticed out of the corner of my eye that Mr. Fujikama had been moved to a room on this ward. So an hour later I stopped in. He lay very still, bed covers perfectly smoothed by his Caucasian wife, a woman who expressed her heartbreak by vigorously keeping everything immaculate. Asking him how he was, I was perplexed at his whispered "I have a mathematical problem." What is the problem? "I won't get in the gate. I may be an hour late, or fifteen minutes late, or three minutes late, but I won't get in the gate." Still puzzled. Why won't you get in the gate? "He won't let me," returned the whisper. Mrs. Fujikama interrupted with the strident urgency of despair, "You'll get in any gate there is!" Who won't let you? The whisper was fading. "Why, Jesus! He's the gatekeeper!" Ah. Now I recognized the guiding hand of the Holy Spirit. "I feel thy finger and find Thee," G. M. Hopkins explains.[11] So as his wife bustled distractedly in another part of the large room, I told once again of the Savior of my soul, the man of Calvary who gave his life for me, the Man of Sorrows who is acquainted with grief, who sees each sparrow fall; of the forgiveness of the cross, the freedom and joy of resurrection (mine in the shadow and efficacy of Christ's), the atonement that waits, even and especially for the dying thief. And of no more pain, no more tears, no more death. His Asian eyes held mine intensely, then he slept.

Next evening, walking again the same hallway and seeing him alone, I went in. The TV racketed away, his wife gone home for dinner. At my soft hello he opened his eyes. Scarcely able to speak and helpless to reach for the TV switch just at arm's length, he nodded me to turn it off. His last whispered words, eyes again closed, lips scarcely moving, were, "Mathematical question solved. Thank you." Again he slept. A few days later his dear Redeemer welcomed him, face to face.

As Charles Malik says, the university truly is one of the great institutions of the Western world: it produces the accountants, the lawyers, the business folk, the doctors, the engineers—and the high school teachers like Mr. Fujikama. As our eldest son later reminded me, Mr. Fujikama had taught the choir Handel's *Messiah* every year, yet in all those years had not encountered that same Messiah himself. Throughout his university training in mathematics and music he had not stopped to listen to, perhaps was unable to hear, the voice of the Lord. Often the crises of adolescence alert our ears to the small soft voice of Christ, but only at that final crisis in the valley of the shadow of death did Mr. Fujikama seek and was found. He had known and loved Handel's oratorio, he had taught hundreds of young people the voice of the Lord in the Scriptures that Handel set to music, but it took the intimacy of a compassionate fellow being, walking and talking with him in the valley of the shadow, for him to hear the voice of Jesus ("You will be my witnesses," he tells us [Acts 1:8]) voicing forgiveness to him, inviting him to walk together on across the river.

In the Humanities our students hear many voices, all originating from the same Accuser: voices telling them that they are victims. Racial victims, women victims, colonial victims; victims of the

---

11. Hopkins, "The Wreck of the Deutschland," 51.

moralists, victims of the government, victims of their family, victims of the university administration, financial victims, victims of logic, victims of the church. The same voices urge them to rebel: against the government, the men or the women, the family, marriage, business, religion, fashion. Students are encouraged to establish their identity as ones who accuse and fight—fight victimhood, fight the decadent west, fight the establishment. They are indoctrinated by what Robert Irwin in his book *Dangerous Knowledge: Orientalism and Its Discontents*[12] describes as the adversarial mentality so common among students and radical lecturers. The result is alienation and a self-righteous anger that corrodes the soul.

In accomplishing our two tasks, we are latter-day Elijahs sent as the prophet Malachi foretells in the final sentence of Hebrew Scripture, "before the coming of the great and dreadful day of the LORD: [to] turn the heart of the fathers to the children, and the heart of the children to their fathers, lest I [the Lord] come and smite the earth with a curse" (Mal. 4:5–6, KJV). Appropriately, the New Testament begins by tracing back through history the son-father relationships from the birth of the Son of Man all the way back to Adam, the son of God. From that point on it describes the heart of our heavenly Father turning toward his children—"For God so loved the world that he gave his only begotten Son. . . ." (John 3:16, KJV)—and the voice calling out from chapter to chapter to turn our hearts toward the Messiah, who lived, so loved us that "for the joy that was set before him" (Heb. 12:2, KJV) he accepted crucifixion so that we lost souls and distracted minds might find our way home to our heavenly Father. Calling, calling, calling. The New Testament then bears record of the thousands of hearts and minds that heard his voice and turned.

Jesus urges us to voice his gospel throughout the world (Mark 16:15); and he has recently brought the world onto our campuses: every religion, every race, every tongue. We just need to "preach the gospel" here in our own backyard, with the authority of a professorship and the guiding hand of his Holy Spirit. To do so without abusing our authority in a secular institution requires only the winsomeness of our own broken hearts, together with a holy boldness to confess Christ when students come asking. And asking

12. Robert Irwin, *Dangerous Knowledge: Orientalism and Its Discontents* (New York: Overlook Press, 2006).

they do certainly come—although it took me a while to recognize the ever-varying form of the question. Sometimes it is quite blunt, like Kelly's "Sir, why are you a Christian?" or last year Mark's astonishing request as he caught up with me after class and said, "Sir, may I have coffee with you, as you have offered us all today, to make up for the missed class?" Yes of course. Anything in particular on your mind? "Well, sir (Mark is in the Canadian Armed Forces Reserve), I know all about Jesus of course. But I don't know how to be sure that he is in my heart." Shock! When had I ever spoken in class about *that*? "Well, sir, you haven't directly. But I have taken four of your courses by now, you know. . . ." That evening after two hours in a Williams Coffee Pub, Mark plying me with questions, I asked if he wanted to respond to the voice of Jesus right then, eyes wide open looking soberly at each other, following me phrase after phrase. He smartly responded "Yes, sir!" In the eighteen months since that night, watching the growth in faith of this young military man, I have wondered about the mid-sixties couple who sat literally at our elbows on the fixed adjoining seats of the little "foursome" table, prolonging their coffee in complete silence for two hours. Why did the Holy Spirit seat them beside Mark and myself? Were they joining the battle in prayer? Perhaps angels unaware? Or had they never yet heard the voice of the master themselves? Suppose I will have to wait until "that day" when "I shall know even as also I am known" (1 Cor. 13:12, KJV). Other times the question is indirect, or even silent. Stacy is now in the fourth week of the third course she has taken with me—two of them last term. She sits at eye level in a small rising amphitheatre, just to the right of my normal line of vision, in other words, where she can most watch without being watched. Three hours a week she leans forward, motionless, intense with unvoiced questions. Holy Spirit, show me the moment and the answer, for Stacy's sake, and for Christ's.

The president of one of our most acclaimed Canadian universities, himself an English professor and formerly a clergyman, two years ago observed to me, "The Humanities have lost their way in the past two decades." He is not alone in his opinion, for as I write, an e-mail arrives announcing a *Symposium on the Humanities: Finding a Place in Changing Times* at Columbia University. The same e-mail announces *The Fifth International Conference on New Directions in the Humanities* at the American University of Paris. Students seem to be arriving at the same conclusion, voting with their feet by walking away from the humanities so that across North America humanities student registrations drop markedly. Senior undergraduate and graduate students remark to me that they are moving away from English studies because the literature classroom is so heavily politicized, so technology-focused, and because postmodernism and critical theory are so dismissive of the text for its own sake on its own terms that they cannot study literature itself. In other words, our young people are sick of our sickness. Worse, critical theory, with the nihilism and cynicism that Charles Malik denounces so clearly, tells them that every philosophical and religious position is culturally determined, having no ultimate validity. As Christian Terry Eagleton has recently announced in a dramatic late-career about-face,

> Cultural theory as we have it promises to grapple with some fundamental problems, but on the whole fails to deliver. It has been shamefaced about morality and metaphysics, embarrassed about love, biology, religion and revolution, largely silent about evil, reticent about death and suffering, dogmatic about essences, universals and foundations, and superficial about truth, objectivity and disinterestedness.[13]

We have silenced the voices that would speak peace to their souls and wisdom to their minds. As Kafka says in "A Hunger Artist," they find themselves on a hunger strike because the abundant food is not to their taste.[14] Or to change the metaphor, we find ourselves like Elijah, straining our ears in whirlwind, earthquake, and fire, listening for the voice of God, but not hearing it because that voice is a "still small voice." Let the Scripture speak:

> Behold, the LORD passed by, and a great and strong wind rent the mountains, and brake in pieces the rocks before the LORD; but the LORD was not in the wind: and after the wind an earthquake; but the LORD was not in the earthquake: And after the earthquake a fire; but the LORD was not in the fire: and after the fire a still small voice. (1 Kings 19:11–12, KJV)

---

13. Terry Eagleton, *After Theory* (New York: Basic Books, 2003), 101–2.
14. Nahum N. Glarzer, ed., *Franz Kafka: The Complete Stories* (New York: Schocken Books, 1971), 277.

The "canonical" texts within the humanities are rife with the "voice of God" speaking to the "angst of man"—and so often our job is simply to lead students to these texts and allow God's pursuing voice to speak to their hearts.

The Text's the Thing

What is to be done? Emulate Hamlet, who, when confounded by the rottenness of his society, concluded: "The play's the thing / Wherein I'll catch the conscience of the king."[15] Art, and in our case literature, is a powerful voice calling lost souls and minds. So let us return to the text for the text's sake, letting it speak in its own voice, rather than imposing on it the voice of our convictions. The value of reading old books is to discover, ponder, and assess perspectives outside our current ones, perspectives on which our society was built, or perhaps which it abandoned long ago, but not to look upon books first of all as evidence to bolster preconceptions. Christian professors might feel vulnerable at this point lest they be accused of reading books that endorse their Christian views. The simple answer is that for writers such as Chaucer, Spenser, Shakespeare, Donne, Milton—and on and on, through Jane Austen, the Bronte sisters, Christina Rossetti up to T. S. Eliot and Margaret Avison (the much-medaled living Canadian poetess), life and faith in Christ is the presupposition of their work. To read Charles Dickens's *A Tale of Two Cities* and find him juxtaposing the guillotine of the French Revolution with the cross of Christ is not to impose our values on him, it is to understand his. In contrast, at a conference several years ago a young Vassar PhD graduate read a paper in Victorian literature in which she claimed that Dickens is a misogynist, her evidence being that he caricatures women. When in the question period I pointed out that Dickens's device of caricature is common among serial fiction writers, that he used it with all his characters, and that in his novels women come off neither better nor worse than other groups, many in the audience hissed and the chairwoman scolded that questions not assertions were required in the "question" period. A female colleague beside

---

15. *Hamlet*, ed. R. C. Bald (Arlington Heights, IL: Harlan Davidson, 1946), 2.2.590. References are to act, scene, and line.

me whispered, "They all know you are right, of course. That is why they hiss."

Elizabeth Kantor concurs in her recent *The Politically Incorrect Guide to English and American Literature*[16] that English Department students are too often required to read books for evidence to grind axes: postcolonial axes, feminist axes, postmodernist axes, queer theory axes, cultural theory axes, axes, axes. Students need to learn to value the text for the issues it raises and for its artistic methods. For example, to read Shakespeare's *The Taming of the Shrew* as fodder for the feminist cause is to wrench it out of its context, to proudly mock perhaps the greatest dramatist in the history of civilization, and to shut ourselves off from a comprehension of human nature, which, while some might disagree with it, encompasses and distinguishes between Israelite and Gentile authority, which is to say protective and abusive authority, as clearly set out by our Savior himself (Matt. 20:25). The quality of Kate's submission to Petruchio in this uproariously funny farce is profoundly Christian, a submission not to be feared by any woman, and wholly within the best of Christian tradition in its glorification of femininity and the empowerment of wives.

To teach the works of anti-Christian or non-Christian literature in a dispassionate manner, describing its artistic excellence while pointing out contrasts with the literature of Christians—that is to say, by identifying the variety of voices speaking through literature— is not only academically responsible, but is to present "the whole truth" in respect of our responsibility to inform our classes. Such literature might be that of the Greeks, of the Theatre of the Absurd writers, caustic Matthew Arnolds, or atheistic John Stuart Mills. The excellence of these non-Christians is to be wholeheartedly affirmed, whether or not we identify their limitations. To those who argue that the professor's task is to give purely objective presentations without revealing their own biases, I answer first that such a view is naïve, for students delight in quickly recognizing our biases; second, that across the university, both outside and within the humanities, various theories are presented, with the favored ones clearly stated and defended; and third that students itch to hear our own perspectives. Moreover, great educators throughout history

---

16. Elizabeth Kantor, *The Politically Incorrect Guide to English and American Literature* (Washington, DC: Regnery, 2006), 50.

have worn their hearts on their sleeve, as it were; and to present an even-handed treatment of various perspectives is to provide a corrective for the current axe-grinding atmosphere, an air-freshener of sorts. Believing that Jesus Christ is the Way, the Truth, and the Life, competent professors who serve him can affirm with humility that an academically and professionally responsible presentation of any work in the humanities can illuminate that Way, Truth, and Life, even where such a presentation never explicitly mentions Jesus Christ. With the atheist John Stuart Mill we can affirm our faith that truth exists, that mankind can recognize it and will respond as it is clearly presented, that open debate is a primary means of such recognition, and that open debate will raise our hold on truth from superstition to vital comprehension.[17] So we need not fear letting every voice be heard.

But, adds Dr. Kantor, the simple stark facts are that most great literary writers were explicitly Christian.[18] Are we to avoid the Christian convictions of these greats by omitting their Christian writings? Eliot's postconversion poetry and essays? Browning's delineation between hypocritical and true Christians? e. e. Cummings's conversion poem, "i thank you God for most this amazing day"? Tennyson's invocation of Jesus Christ in the opening lines of *In Memoriam*, which is probably the poem most widely acclaimed within the lifetime of its author in the entire history of English literature, rapidly translated into nine languages? His opening prayer, read and acclaimed by millions of his contemporaries, begins:

> Strong Son of God, immortal Love,
> Whom we, that have not seen thy face,
> By faith, and faith alone, embrace,
> Believing where we can not prove. . . .

Of all the works of literature which record of the salvation of its author's soul and mind, this is surely one of the greatest, by the greatest poet of his century. It is all too rarely taught.

This past year when I told a graduate seminar that they were to read the prose writings of John Ruskin without looking at a single

---

17. In *On Liberty,* Mill presents this now classical argument in defense of freedom of speech. See John Stuart Mill, *On Liberty,* ed. David Spitz (New York: Norton, 1975).

18. Kantor, *Politically Incorrect Guide,* 5.

secondary source, and to come back each week with half a dozen pages of summary and response, the class confessed to being panic-stricken, and one abruptly withdrew for that single reason. How can one expect otherwise? The critical theory that they are all required to master sneers that every text is unreliable; that only the theorist's assertions are valid; that the student's task is to master and echo the opinions of theorists, not to hold opinions of their own, unless such opinions are echoes of the theorists', and, in a remarkably self-contradictory claim, that there is no absolute truth.

The text's the thing, not only in English but also in religious studies, history, the ancient and modern languages, and so on. Students taking my course in Literature and the Bible have often said, "Sir, in the Religious Studies program we could only find courses on various views about the Bible; we could find none in which we could read and study the Bible itself." In the History Department one device separating fathers and sons has been to abandon pre-twentieth-century history, which includes the history of Christianity. So in many universities it is possible to obtain a BA in history without having taken any courses prior to 1850; in some universities, prior to 1950. In other words, to separate the fathers from the children, the children from the fathers. How appropriate that the New Testament begins with two genealogies, family histories of fathers and sons from Joseph backward and forward to Adam. How better to begin the record of the Messiah turning the hearts of our heavenly Father to his children and his children to their heavenly Father. So we can begin countering the Accuser by returning to a study of the last two thousand years and earlier, which will include the entire history of Christ in the church and the church in the world.

Philosophy: "The Enclosing Cage of Reason"

Peter Kreeft may well be right when he observes in chapter 4 that English and History are the most corrupt departments in the Humanities. They are the two disciplines in which the most dramatic reactions against Christ have multiplied. But for professor of Philosophy Charles Malik, writing in *The Wonder of Being*, Philosophy too is barren. Listen:

> The fact that philosophical systems historically knock each other out was clearly seen by Kant and Hegel, who nevertheless were themselves

sucked into the immanent process of the history of philosophy and
could not liberate themselves into genuine transcendence. They simply
succeeded in depositing themselves as links in the endless chain of
thought. . . . [But they kick] against the enclosing cage of reason. These
men are not to be taken very seriously. . . . What an incredible jolt
your whole being undergoes when you come to the Bible or attend the
Divine Liturgy or have an intimate personal chat with a friend after
reading or lecturing on the sublimest philosophy—that of Plato or
Aristotle or Kant or Hegel! The philosophers are worth nothing so far
as being and existence are concerned compared to one passage from
the word of God—a Psalm or a chapter from Paul or the Gospels—or
to a genuine moment of living and free communication with a friend.
This existential jolt is the most terrible experience I know in my life.
Supposing you really know what David or Paul or Jesus Christ is
talking about so far as your own living-dying existence is concerned—
how can you then take any of the philosophers seriously?[19]

Yet even in Philosophy, the discipline in which Charles Malik
flourished at Harvard and Freiburg before moving into international
politics, the voice of Jesus calls, for "Christ plays in ten thousand
places" (again in Hopkins's words).[20]

Here is Jacqueline, a young colleague of mine. Growing up in
a non-practicing Roman Catholic French Canadian family, she
developed an interest in drama and began her own troupe. At Laval
University she took a philosophy course, and was introduced by a
Christian professor to Thomas Aquinas. This young Québécois, as
we say in Canada, soon followed the footprints of Aquinas right into
the kingdom of Heaven. Good-bye Drama, Hello Philosophy. She
flourished, completed a Princeton post-doc, accepted an assistant
professorship, and was straight-way asked to co-teach a course
on female genital mutilation south of the Sahara. Wide-eyed and
wrinkle-browed, Jacqueline exclaims in her fascinating French-
Canadian accent (I chuckle to hear her students using philosophical
terms with a French accent!), "I never imagined a professor of
medieval philosophy would be expected to lecture on such a thing!"
She wrestles on other fronts too:

19. Charles Malik, *The Wonder of Being* (Waco, Texas: Word Books, 1974),
34–35.
20. G. M. Hopkins, "As Kingfishers Catch Fire," in *The Poems of Gerard
Manley Hopkins*, ed. W. H. Gardner and N. H. Mackenzie (London: Oxford University Press, 1967), 90.

Philosophy Academics often assume that in order to establish his conclusions, the Christian philosopher necessarily relies on principles that come from his religion, and that therefore, they do not have purely scientific worth outside of theology. This is exactly why many specialists in Ancient Greek philosophy refuse to consult Aquinas. They act as if his faith invalidated his natural, rational capacity, whereas it is precisely the opposite that happens. Christian philosophers and intellectuals in general can be helped in their natural endeavors by the fact that they have faith, insofar as it gives them more stable and ordered lives, more hope and more courage, and insofar as grace might sometimes operate to give their intellect some supplementary light to understand difficult things better. But as far as they clearly keep in mind that they must always explain things in terms of causes that they have grasped with their natural reason and based on the evidence—with or without the help of God, as long as their explanations of things is natural, the work they accomplish is as solid as the work of non-Christians (if not better).

I suppose that the difficulty is particularly acute for the Christian philosopher, more than for the Christian chemist or physicist or even the Christian historian or sociologist, because of the proximity of the objects of theology and of philosophy, and because of the fact it is part of the philosophical endeavor to reflect about the first causes of the universe. I suppose also that the situation is in part due to the fact that nowadays many faculty members and students have never even heard about the possibility of conducting a natural reflection about God, let alone experienced it. Certainly, Christian philosophers would profit from making the distinction between the two kinds of theology, natural and revealed, better known and to give examples of conclusions about God that can be reached naturally. Then people would at least be aware of the possibility for a Christian philosopher to think about the great questions of origins in terms of causes and concepts which are also accessible to a non-Christian.

Charles Malik's comment on this eleventh-century philosopher is: "St. Thomas Aquinas faced head on this question of the seeming contradiction between God's goodness and omnipotence as 'proving' that God does not exist, and showed, basing himself on Augustine, that 'part of the infinite goodness of God (is) that He should allow evil to exist, and out of it produce good.'"[21]

Hello, Jacqueline. How might students discover Christ in a philosophy classroom?

21. Malik, *Wonder of Being*, 27.

Hi John. I enjoyed lunch with [your wife] Roberta today. I think she's lovely. First, as to how a student reading philosophy might encounter God, there are certainly a few ways. (One could not directly encounter Christ, since he is not an object of philosophy, although the road to such an encounter might be prepared). Philosophy might be favorable, as would be other life situations in which one makes a sincere effort to know the truth and to be true. Second, I would definitely advise going straight to Aquinas. Third, it seems to me there are two ways for a teacher to direct someone toward Christ; either you refer to your personal life and experience as a human being—some teachers of mine did do that with me and it had its effect; it certainly impressed me a lot as a student that all the people I thought were intelligent and brilliant happened to be such ardent believers; or, as I explained before, he might present the student with the possibility of a reflection about God on purely natural grounds.

So in Philosophy too, the text's the thing in the winning of mind and souls. Jacqueline faces adversity in the classroom, commonly from young men who attack her presentation of the Christian stance of such as Aquinas and one of his most articulate twentieth-century expositors, the German philosopher Josef Pieper. T. S. Eliot, in his introduction to Pieper's *Leisure the Basis of Culture*, prophesied that Pieper would bring philosophy back to the layman. Now half a century later, Eliot's prophesy has come true, Pieper having written dozens of books and having been translated into many languages. Yet Jacqueline has a devoted majority of students who thrive under her instruction. Significantly, the objectors quiet down once the class moves back to pre-Christian philosophy.

Conclusion

And so it goes for each of the humanities disciplines. Lear's cry, "Who will tell me who I am?" is an echo of Moses' query to the Lord, "Who are you?" (cf. Ex. 3:13–14) and of Jesus' question to Peter, "Who do you say that I am?" Peter's answer, "The Christ of God" (Luke 9:20) came after Peter had been a follower for many months, and after Peter had heard Jesus' voice telling him who he himself was: Cephas, a rock. Here is the backdrop for that ancient Christian tradition of baptism, or "Christening" and the giving of a "Christian" name. Peter's experience is echoed by the demoniac, who begins with "What do you want with me, Jesus, Son of the Most High God?" To the demoniac Jesus answers, "What is your name?" The reply, "We are many" (Mark 5:6–10), comes from the legion of demons tormenting this man who has been rejected everywhere, and has become a self-tormenter. This same Jesus disposes of the many demonic voices, so that the man is found clean, clothcd, in his right mind, and at peace. As a consequence, Jesus is asked to vacate the territory by those who prefer the demonic voices (see Mark 5:11–17). It is still the case in our universities. But let you and me pray together,

> I do not hide your righteousness in my heart;
> I speak of your faithfulness and salvation.
> I do not conceal your love and your truth
> from the great assembly. Psalm 40:10

Discussion Questions

1. What are the "canonical" texts within your discipline? How is God's voice manifest within these texts? How is the human condition manifest within these texts?

2. What are some of the loudest voices, or messages, communicated to students in your discipline?

3. What are some of the ways you sustain your walk with God so that you are "prepared to give an account" of your faith?

4. Who are the Christian intellectuals within your discipline—past and contemporary?

5. How is your discipline affected by postmodernism?

6. Do you agree with Malik that nothing in philosophy, or your own discipline, compares in being or experience to the Word of God or an intimate connection with a friend? If so, how could this insight affect your teaching and interaction with students and colleagues?

7. How did you *first* hear the voice of God in your life?

8. How do you *now* "hear" the voice of God? How can you help your students hear God's voice over all the competing voices?

8

CONCLUDING THOUGHTS ON THE TWO TASKS OF THE CHRISTIAN SCHOLAR

WILLIAM LANE CRAIG

The Battle

"The contemporary Western intellectual world," writes the noted philosopher Alvin Plantinga, "is a battleground or arena in which rages a battle for men's souls."[1] Christian academics, especially those who teach at secular institutions, are the church's front line in this battle.

It is the common conviction of the contributors to this volume that this is a front that is absolutely crucial for the advance of the kingdom of God in our day. Why? Simply because the single most important institution shaping Western culture is the university. It is at the university that our future political leaders, our journalists, our lawyers, our teachers, our business executives, our artists, will be

---

1. Alvin Plantinga, "The Twin Pillars of Christian Scholarship" in *Seeking Understanding: The Stob Lectures 1986–1998* (Grand Rapids: Eerdmans, 2001), 124.

trained. It is at the university that they will formulate or, more likely, simply absorb the worldview that will shape their lives. And since these are the opinion makers and leaders who shape our culture, the worldview that they imbibe at the university will be the one that shapes our culture. If we change the university, we change our culture through those who shape culture. If the Christian worldview can be restored to a place of prominence and respect at the university, it will have a leavening effect throughout society.

Why is this important? Simply because the gospel is never heard in isolation. It is always heard against the background of the cultural milieu in which one lives. A person raised in a cultural milieu in which Christianity is still seen as an intellectually viable option will display an openness to the gospel that a person who is secularized will not. For the secular person you may as well tell him to believe in fairies or leprechauns as in Jesus Christ! Or, to give a more realistic illustration, it is like a devotee of the Hare Krishna movement approaching you on the street and inviting you to believe in Krishna. Such an invitation strikes us as bizarre, freakish, even amusing. But to a person on the streets of Delhi, such an invitation would, I assume, appear quite reasonable and be cause for reflection. I fear that evangelicals may appear almost as weird to persons on the streets of Bonn, Stockholm, or New York as do the devotees of Krishna.[2]

The Need for Christian Scholars

It is part of the task of Christian academics to help create and sustain a cultural milieu in which the gospel can be heard as an intellectually viable option for thinking men and women. The great Princeton theologian J. Gresham Machen rightly declared:

> False ideas are the greatest obstacles to the reception of the gospel. We may preach with all the fervor of a reformer and yet succeed only in winning a straggler here and there, if we permit the whole collective thought of the nation to be controlled by ideas which prevent Christianity from being regarded as anything more than a harmless

---

2. For evidence, see Sam Schulman, "Without God, Gall Is Permitted," *Wall Street Journal*, January 5, 2007, W11.

delusion. Under such circumstances, what God desires us to do is to destroy the obstacle at its root.[3]

The root of the obstacle is to be found in the university, and it is there that it must be attacked. We desperately need evangelical scholars who can compete with secular scholars on their own terms of scholarship. Recall Charles Malik's warning to American Christians of the danger of neglecting the mind. He asked pointedly:

Who among the evangelicals can stand up to the great secular . . . scholars on their own terms of scholarship and research? Who among evangelical scholars is quoted as a normative source by the greatest secular authorities on history or philosophy or psychology or sociology or politics? Does your mode of thinking have the slightest chance of becoming the dominant mode in the great universities of Europe and America which stamp your entire civilization with their spirit and ideas?[4]

Malik went on to say:

It will take a different spirit altogether to overcome this great danger. . . . As an example only, I say this different spirit, so far as the domain of philosophy alone is concerned, which is the most important domain so far as thought and intellect are concerned, must see the tremendous value of spending a whole year doing nothing except poring intensely over the *Republic* or the *Sophist* of Plato, or two years over the *Metaphysics* or the *Ethics* of Aristotle, or three years over the *City of God* of Augustine. Even if you start now on a crash program in this and other domains, it will be a century at least before you catch up with the Harvards and Tübingens and the Sorbonnes, and think of where these universities will be then. For the sake of greater effectiveness in witnessing to Jesus Christ himself, as well as for their own sakes, the evangelicals cannot afford to keep on living on the periphery of responsible intellectual existence.[5]

---

3. Address delivered on September 20, 1912, at the opening of the 101st session of Princeton Theological Seminary. Reprinted in J. Gresham Machen, *What Is Christianity?* (Grand Rapids: Eerdmans, 1951), 162.
4. See page 64 in chapter 2.
5. Ibid.

These words hit like a hammer. Evangelicals have for the most part been living on the periphery of responsible intellectual existence. Where are the Christian historians, literary critics, physicists, sociologists? As Christian academics, we need to examine ourselves to see if we are contending effectively for the faith in our area. If the university and, as a consequence, our culture is to be changed, evangelical academics need to exercise a leavening influence for Christ in their respective fields of expertise.

The Transformation of a Discipline

It can be done! For example, over the last forty years there has been an ongoing revolution in the Anglo-American world in the field of philosophy. Since the late 1960s Christian philosophers have been coming out of the closet and defending the truth of the Christian worldview with philosophically sophisticated arguments in the finest secular journals and societies. And the face of Anglo-American philosophy has been transformed as a result.

Fifty years ago philosophers widely regarded talk about God as literally *meaningless*, as mere gibberish, but today no informed philosopher could take such a viewpoint. In fact, many of America's finest philosophers today are outspoken Christians.

To give you a feel for the impact of this revolution, I want to quote at some length from an article that appeared in the fall of 2001 in the journal *Philo* lamenting what the author called "the desecularization of academia that evolved in philosophy departments since the late 1960s." The author, himself a prominent atheist philosopher, writes:

> By the second half of the twentieth century, universities . . . had been become in the main secularized. The standard . . . position in each field . . . assumed or involved arguments for a naturalist world-view; departments of theology or religion aimed to understand the meaning and origins of religious writings, not to develop arguments against naturalism. Analytic philosophers . . . treated theism as an anti-realist or non-cognitivist world-view, requiring the reality, not of a deity, but merely of emotive expressions or certain "forms of life." . . .
>
> This is not to say that none of the scholars in the various academic fields were realist theists in their "private lives"; but realist theists, for the most part, excluded their theism from their publications and teaching, in large part because theism . . . was mainly considered to

have such a low epistemic status that it did not meet the standards of an "academically respectable" position to hold. The secularization of mainstream academia began to quickly unravel upon the publication of Plantinga's influential book, *God and Other Minds*, in 1967. It became apparent to the philosophical profession that this book displayed that realist theists were not outmatched by naturalists in terms of the most valued standards of analytic philosophy: conceptual precision, rigor of argumentation, technical erudition, and an in-depth defense of an original world-view. This book, followed seven years later by Plantinga's even more impressive book, *The Nature of Necessity*, made it manifest that a realist theist was writing at the highest qualitative level of analytic philosophy, on the same playing field as Carnap, Russell, Moore, Grünbaum, and other naturalists. . . .

Naturalists passively watched as realist versions of theism, most influenced by Plantinga's writings, began to sweep through the philosophical community, until today perhaps one-quarter or one-third of philosophy professors are theists, with most being orthodox Christians. Although many theists do not work in the area of the philosophy of religion, so many of them do work in this area that there are now over five philosophy journals devoted to theism or the philosophy of religion, such as *Faith and Philosophy*, *Religious Studies*, *International Journal of the Philosophy of Religion*, *Sophia*, *Philosophia Christi*, etc. *Philosophia Christi* began in the late 1990s and already is overflowing with submissions from leading philosophers. . . . Theists in other fields tend to compartmentalize their theistic beliefs from their scholarly work; they rarely assume and never argue for theism in their scholarly work. If they did, they would be committing academic suicide or, more exactly, their articles would quickly be rejected. . . . But in philosophy, it became, almost overnight, "academically respectable" to argue for theism, making philosophy a favored field of entry for the most intelligent and talented theists entering academia today.[6]

He concludes:

God is not "dead" in academia; he returned to life in the late 1960s and is now alive and well in his last academic stronghold, philosophy departments.[7]

---

6. Quentin Smith, "The Metaphilosophy of Naturalism," *Philo* 4, no. 2 (2001): 3–4.

7. Ibid., 4.

This is the testimony of a prominent atheist philosopher to the change that has taken place before his eyes in Anglo-American philosophy. I think that he is probably exaggerating when he estimates that one-quarter to one-third of American philosophers are theists, but what his estimates do reveal is the *perceived impact* of Christian philosophers upon this field. Like Gideon's army, a committed minority of activists can have an impact far out of proportion to its numbers. The principal error that he makes is calling philosophy departments God's "last stronghold" at the university. On the contrary, philosophy departments are a beachhead, from which operations can be launched to impact other disciplines at the university for Christ.

The point is that the task of desecularization is not hopeless or impossible, nor need significant changes take as long to achieve as one might think. It is this sort of Christian scholarship that represents the best hope for the transformation of culture that Malik and Machen envisioned, and its true impact for the cause of Christ will be felt only in the next generation, as it filters down into popular culture.

Advice for Christian Professors

So what positive suggestions might one offer to help Christian academics to be more effective in their battle for the souls of men and women being waged at the university? Let me make three suggestions:

1. *Engage intellectually not just with your chosen discipline, but with your Christian faith.* It seems strange to have to make this suggestion to Christian academics. You would think that as persons who have chosen the life of the mind as their vocation, they would be naturally intellectually curious and so desirous of understanding and exploring Christian theology and apologetics. Of all people, you would expect them to be intellectually engaged with their faith!

But I have found that this is not at all the case. I am astonished at what a weak grasp many Christian professors seem to have of Christian doctrine and how impotent they are when called upon to give a defense for the hope that is in them (1 Peter 3:15). One would expect non-Christian professors to be largely ignorant of Christian theology. After all, we all specialize in a certain field and as a result are ignorant of things in other fields. For example, I know something about philosophy; but I know absolutely nothing about economics, or chemical engineering, or agriculture, or business. What is shocking to me, however, is how many Christian academics seem content to possess a profound knowledge of their area of specialization and yet have little better than a Sunday school education when it comes to their Christian faith, on which they have staked their lives and eternal destiny.

I have been stunned by conversations with Christian professors that reveal that they have little grasp of basic Christian doctrines such as the Trinity, the two natures of Christ, or the attributes of God. It also surprises me when I see their loss for words when called upon to explain why they believe that Christianity is true. Though brilliant in their chosen fields, they are like uninformed laymen when it comes to their Christian faith.

"My beloved brethren, these things ought not to be," to quote the apostle Paul. I'm obviously not saying that every Christian academic needs to become a theologian. But I am saying that we need to have a fundamental grasp of basic Christian doctrine, church history, Old and New Testament contents, and apologetics. Really, all this would involve is digesting a few good books on these areas.

To be practical let me recommend a few books to get you started. On New Testament introduction, try Donald Guthrie's *New Testament Introduction* or Carson, Moo, and Morris's *Introduction to the New Testament*. For Christian doctrine, I recommend Hubert Cunliffe-Jones's *A History of Christian Doctrine* or Roger Olson's *The Story of Christian Theology*. And for basic apologetics, start with Lee Strobel's popular *Case for a Creator* and *Case for Christ* or my own *Reasonable Faith*.

There is simply no excuse for Christian academics, who have devoted themselves to the life of the mind, to be lazy and ignorant when it comes to the truth claims of the Christian religion. We shall be far sharper tools in the Lord's hand if we engage our minds intellectually with our own Christian faith.

2. *Strive to integrate your Christian faith with your discipline.* As educated Christians our goal should be to have a Christian weltanschauung, a world and life view that provides a Christian perspective on the arts, on physics, on literature, on business, and so on. All truth is God's truth, so no area of study lies outside the domain of God's truth. Somehow it is all integrated into the whole, which is perfectly known by God alone. Our goal should be to seek

to discover how our field of study fits into the whole scheme of God's truth.

What that implies is that we must be prepared to think Christianly about our area of specialization. Here it is absolutely crucial to realize in a very self-conscious way that the presuppositions which underlie our chosen discipline will have been very largely shaped by secular, naturalistic worldviews. Therefore, as Christians we shall have to be prepared to re-think our whole discipline from the ground up in line with Christian presuppositions.

For example, I am convinced that virtually the whole of twentieth-century physics has been derouted by the defective epistemology of verificationism, and therefore is drastically in need of being rethought on the basis of different epistemological assumptions. Verificationism was a philosophy popular in the first half of the twentieth century that held that only sentences which are empirically verifiable are meaningful. Notice that the verificationism of which I speak is a theory of meaning, not a test for truth. Empirical verification is vital in testing the truth of scientific theories, but verificationism held that any sentence that cannot be empirically verified is not even false; it is meaningless. Verificationism sprang out of a naturalistic worldview that wants nothing to do with anything metaphysical, or beyond the physical. On this basis statements about non-empirical realities such as God or moral values were dismissed as meaningless nonsense.

The central pillars of twentieth-century physics, relativity theory and quantum theory, are both based on a philosophy of verificationism. It was only on this basis that Einstein could dismiss the reality of absolute time, absolute space, and absolute simultaneity. Since these entities could not be detected empirically, Einstein brushed them aside as meaningless and substituted in their place operational definitions of these key concepts, which issue in a radically different view of the world. Those who rejected the epistemology of verificationism, such as H. A. Lorentz, took a quite different interpretation of the equations that lie at the heart of special relativity. Lorentz's interpretation affirmed the reality of absolute simultaneity and of length, even if these quantities are empirically undetectable by us.

Similarly, in quantum physics Heisenberg's indeterminacy principle was predicated on the same verificationist epistemology. Since the position and momentum of a subatomic particle cannot be simultaneously measured, such quantities were said not to exist independently of measurements. Physicists who rejected verificationism, such as Louis de Broglie or David Bohm, offered quite different physical interpretations of the equations of quantum theory than those accepted in the standard Copenhagen interpretation. When Einstein himself protested that our ignorance of such quantities as the position and momentum of a subatomic particle doesn't imply that they do not exist, Heisenberg rightly replied that he was only employing the same epistemology that lay at the foundations of Einstein's own theory. Einstein could only retort that a good joke shouldn't be repeated twice!

Indeed, from a Christian point of view verificationism is a joke. For if God exists, then obviously he isn't bound by the finite velocity of light signals and so could know what events were occurring absolutely simultaneously with one another throughout the universe. Nor is his knowledge of the subatomic realm mediated by physical measurement procedures, so that it is no problem at all for him to know what position and momentum is possessed by every elementary particle in the whole of his creation.

Thus the twin pillars of contemporary physics as conventionally understood rest on the rotted timbers of verificationism. What is especially ironic about this situation is that verificationism came under such sustained attack by epistemologists and philosophers of science during the latter half of the twentieth century that it has now been virtually universally abandoned. And yet the theories erected upon its foundation continue on as though nothing had changed. The time is ripe for a radical rethinking of physics from a non-verificationist point of view.

I have been scandalized by the lack of integrative thinking on the part of Christian colleagues. For example, I spoke at length with a Christian professor of literature at one of our state universities who told me that she believed that texts have no meaning. Rather, meaning exists only in the mind of the reader. I was astonished that an intelligent Christian could have bought into the relativistic, postmodern view of meaning that is rampant in departments of English and Literature. I asked her what her view implied for the Bible. As a text does it have no meaning? Is anyone free to give whatever meaning he wants to the biblical text? Is it legitimate to take the meaning of the Bible to be that God is hate and will send everyone to hell who believes in Christ? Could the meaning of the Bible be a play-by-play account of the 2002 World Cup final? She said she exempted the Bible from having no objective meaning because it alone is inspired by God. But I pointed out to her that this move was entirely ad hoc; on the level of text it is just like any other text, regardless of who its author was, and therefore should be objectively meaningless. Thank God that she was enough of a Christian to realize that that conclusion was theologically unacceptable!

She was clearly shaken by our conversation. "I'm going to have to rethink everything," she said. "You see, I've been on the board of a library that was faced with the issue of whether to ban pornographic materials from being available in the library. I argued that since texts have no meaning in themselves and meaning is only in the mind of the reader, nothing is inherently pornographic and that therefore the library should make such materials available. If you're right, then I've made a terrible mistake."

To think that a Christian academic, infected by postmodernism and insufficiently reflective from a Christian point of view, should have thus been responsible for putting pornography in the hands of children and maybe even predators, brought home to me as never before the importance of developing a Christian world and life view, even if that means rethinking the very foundations of our discipline and reforming them in line with Christian truth.

Integrative thinking for most of us will not involve the nuts-and-bolts of our discipline—I mean the routine, day-to-day activities in our field—so much as the philosophy of our discipline. Now I don't expect you all to become philosophers. But you really do need to read something on the philosophy of your field. You need to read some philosophy of education or some business ethics or some philosophy of science or some philosophy of history. Virtually every discipline has a philosophical component of which you, as a Christian academic in that field, need to be aware. This isn't too much to ask; on the contrary, it will make you a better scholar in your field if you understand some of the basic philosophy of your subject.

And what you discover may surprise you! For example, what could be seemingly more neutral than mathematics? How could being a Christian possibly make any difference at all in this field? You'd be surprised. I'm told that most practicing mathematicians are almost unconsciously Platonists. That is to say, they just assume that abstract objects like numbers and sets actually exist as mind-independent realities. But Platonism is, I think, a deeply anti-Christian metaphysic. For such abstract objects are usually conceived to exist necessarily, beyond space and time. These objects exist as uncreated entities, and there are infinities of infinities of infinities of them. But what does this imply for the Christian doctrine of creation and for the divine attribute of aseity? On Platonism God is reduced to but one necessary being among many, an infinitesimal part of reality, most of which exists utterly independently of him. Such a metaphysical pluralism seems incompatible with the Christian doctrine of God who alone exists necessarily and eternally and is the Creator of all reality outside himself. Christian thinkers need to articulate a view of mathematical objects that is consistent with Christian theism.

As Christian academics we cannot afford to be unreflective and simply absorb uncritically the common presuppositions of our discipline, for these may be antithetical to a Christian weltanschauung. Nor should we allow ourselves to be cowed by the prevailing views in our field or afraid to march to the beat of a different drummer. We are to seek the praise of God and not men. And that means thinking integratively as Christians about our chosen field.

3. *Be mindful of your personal, spiritual formation.* In the end the most important thing is not what you do, but who you are. The academic life is inherently an agonistic life. That is to say, it is combative, involving a struggle of ideas. It tends to promote selfish ambition, arrogance, and competitiveness. I recall one scientist who remarked that science is a field where egotistical motivations and the advance of the discipline happen fortunately to coincide!

But this is not the kind of wisdom that God treasures. On the contrary, he calls it demonic. Look at James 3:13–15: "Who is wise and understanding among you? Let him show it by his good life, by deeds done in the humility that comes from wisdom. But if you harbor bitter envy and selfish ambition in your hearts, do not boast about it or deny the truth. Such 'wisdom' does not come down from heaven but is earthly, unspiritual, of the devil." Notice the progression: "earthly, unspiritual, of the devil." This sort of worldly, demonic wisdom is personally destructive, both to you and to others about you.

I recall meeting a scientist in Germany who was separated from his wife and longed to visit his little son. He told us that early on in his career all he could think about was his research, and he invested the best part of his energy and time in pursuing his career. It led to the destruction of his marriage and the loss of his family. "I was a fool!" he told us.

Some of you are probably making this same mistake. I implore you for the sake of Christ to repent, to go to your spouse and to ask forgiveness, and to ask if you together might begin anew. But this must be a serious offer, involving a readiness to cut back on time at work, to give more attention to personal time together, to be willing to give up academic fame and success for the sake of your spouse.

In general, we as Christian academics are called to the same holiness of life to which all disciples of Christ are called. It is vitally important that, as a public representative of Christ, each of us be a person who goes often to his knees to spend time with God, who depends daily on the filling of the Holy Spirit to live a life pleasing and acceptable to God. We must seek Christ's glory, not our own. We must be open to criticism and willing to see our own shortcomings, to learn from our critics. We must not place our career or studies ahead of our family, but rather be prepared to give up our studies and even our career if necessary for the sake of those we love. We must guard against sin, especially sexual sin, in thought as well as deed, so as not to dishonor Christ. We must learn what it means, not to merely *do* things for God, but to *be* the person God wants us to be.

Unless we learn to be who God wants us to be, all our vaunted academic achievements will be as wood, hay, and stubble. Our spiritual formation is therefore as vitally important as our academic formation as Christian faculty.

Conclusion

In summary, we Christian academics stand on the church's front line in one of the most important theaters in the culture war, that of the university. Will you be an effective soldier of Jesus Christ, or will you desert his cause? To be as effective as you can, you need to engage intellectually, not just with your chosen discipline, but with your Christian faith; to strive to integrate your Christian faith with your discipline; and to be mindful of your personal, spiritual formation. May God raise up a mighty force of committed men and women to transform the university and, hence, our culture in such a way that the gospel may be heard afresh in all its life-changing power!

Discussion Questions

1. How is your university and academic discipline shaping the worldview and values of the culture?

2. Philosophy, Dr. Craig asserts, has become a "beachhead, from which operations can be launched to impact other disciplines at the university for Christ."

   - Have you considered the philosophical underpinnings of your discipline and compared them with a Christian perspective?
   - How has this helped you understand the relationship between your discipline and a Christian worldview?
   - How could a transformation happen in your field?
   - What might that transformation look like?

3. Dr. Craig writes that "many Christian academics seem content to possess a profound knowledge of their area of specialization and yet have little better than a Sunday school education when it comes to their Christian faith, on which they have staked their lives and eternal destiny."

   Rate on a scale of 1–10 your understanding of basic Christian doctrines such as:

   - the Trinity
   - the divinity of Christ
   - the attributes of God
   - the resurrection
   - the virgin birth
   - the authority and inspiration of Scripture
   - Christ's substitutionary atonement

   Rate on a scale of 1–10:

   - Your ability to defend these doctrines "with gentleness and respect" (1 Peter 3:15).
   - Your ability to teach these truths to students, colleagues, family, and church members.
   - Your ability to clearly and concisely present and explain the gospel, including an invitation to commit one's life to Jesus Christ.

4. Is a Christian perspective an integral part of your teaching and research? How?

5. Can you discern a naturalistic philosophy in your discipline? If so, contrast it with your Christian worldview and values.

6. "The academic life is inherently an agonistic life. . . . It tends to promote selfish ambition, arrogance, and competitiveness."

   • Has academia become your god, or is God first in your life?

   • What spiritual disciplines and practices do you have that strengthen your relationship with Christ?

   • How would you rate the quality of your relationship with Jesus Christ right now?

   • How well would you say you rely on God's power to live your daily life?

   • Could you easily and clearly explain to a student, colleague, friend, or church member how to be filled with the Holy Spirit and walk daily in his power?

GENERAL INDEX

SCRIPTURE INDEX

199

Professors Who Love And Follow Christ Are Our Heroes

Most movements are born simply,
in the hearts of a few.

For these individuals, the world
is no longer what it once appeared to be.

The compelling cause and person of
Jesus Christ now shines above all else.

Faculty Commons is part of the global faculty network of
Campus Crusade for Christ. On campuses all over the world
we gather as a "transformed minority": men and women who
love the academy, who find the person and works of Jesus of
Nazareth to be satisfying and true, and who look to Him as the
beautiful hope for the world.

We dream of the day when:

- There are movements of Christian professors on
  every campus.

- Every student knows professors who follow Christ
  and point others to Him.

- Christian scholars engage every academic discipline
  so that Christian perspectives are heard and respected.

FACULTY COMMONS
CONNECTING PROFESSORS TO HELP CHANGE THE WORLD

P.O. Box 129, Addison, TX 75001   972-713-7130
w w w . f a c u l t y c o m m o n s . c o m